Maria E. Tifft

A Partial Record of the Descendants of John Tefft of Portsmouth

Maria E. Tifft

A Partial Record of the Descendants of John Tefft of Portsmouth

ISBN/EAN: 9783744727013

Printed in Europe, USA, Canada, Australia, Japan

Cover: Foto ©Andreas Hilbeck / pixelio.de

More available books at **www.hansebooks.com**

A PARTIAL RECORD OF THE DESCENDANTS OF JOHN TEFFT, OF PORTSMOUTH, RHODE ISLAND AND THE NEARLY COMPLETE RECORD OF THE DESCENDANTS OF JOHN TIFFT, OF NASSAU, NEW YORK

Containing the Names of Seven Hundred and Four Descendants, and extending over a period of Two Hundred and Forty-one Years in America Together with other Miscellaneous Records

Compiled by
MARIA E. (MAXON) TIFFT
Buffalo, New York
March, 1896

THE PETER PAUL BOOK COMPANY PUBLISHERS
420 MAIN STREET BUFFALO, NEW YORK 1896

INTRODUCTION

It was not the original intention to compile this genealogy, but so much of the early history was obtained for the inscription on the Tifft monument erected in May, 1895, in Nassau, N. Y., that it was determined to arrange in as compact a form as possible, all the facts learned about the various descendants, in order to preserve the same for future reference.

The record, though incomplete, represents a great deal of labor and study, and is the result of extended examinations of town histories, various family records and genealogies, and also extensive correspondence with the numerous descendants of John Tifft.

An effort has been made to ascertain when the Tiffts came from England and from what part, but so far without success. Two brothers are found in this country; William, in Boston, in 1638, who died leaving only one daughter, and John, of Portsmouth, R. I., in 1655, who is the ancestor of the Rhode Island Tiffts.

The name "Tefft" or "Teft" is Saxon, and means "a piece of ground where there has been a house." (Etymological Dictionary of family and Christian names by William Arthur, A. M.)

The name at different times in Colonial Records is variously spelled,—Teffe, Teft, Tefft, Tieft, Tift and Tifft, all pertaining to the same general family.

The following is an abstract from a letter written by Rev. Benjamin F. Tefft, D. D., LL. D., to Parker W. Tefft of Chicago.

"While in London on a mission for the United States Government, I employed some one to hunt up the family name in England. The result was the following: The family originally belonged to the French Huguenots, when the spelling of the name was "Thevet," and pronounced as if spelled "Tevay." The family with many others were driven out of France

by the St. Bartholomew massacre, and came to England. The Teffts of this country undoubtedly came from England. Now, when you take the name Thevet with its French pronunciation, and put it beside the name of William Teffe, how natural the transition and then how easy to change the final e to t, and produce a name of one syllable and easily pronounced Tifft."

The above mentioned Benjamin F. Tefft was born in Floyd, N. Y., August 20, 1813, and died a few years ago in Bangor, Maine. He was a prominent Methodist Episcopal clergyman, author and teacher. In 1843 he was Professor of Greek and Hebrew Languages in the Indiana Asbury University; in 1846, he was editor of the *Ladies' Repository*, and of the publications of the Western Book Concern. In 1859 he re-entered the itinerant work of the church, and received appointments in Maine. In 1861 he was appointed Chaplain to the First Regiment of Maine Cavalry, Army of the Potomac. In 1862, Consul of the United States to Stockholm, and acting Minister to Sweden. In 1864, Commissioner of Immigration from the north of Europe to the State of Maine. In 1874, representative from Penobscot County to the State Legislature. Dr. Tefft was a member of the Geographical and Statistical Society of New York, and of the Society of Arts of England.

The system of numbering is as follows:

Beginning with John, the names are all numbered consecutively; his oldest child being number 2, and so on. This consecutive numbering precedes the name, and the Roman characters denote the order of births in each family. The small figure following the name denotes the generation.

For example—taking 186 (II) John^6 (who is the descendant that came to Nassau, N. Y., in 1793); going back until we come to this number 186 (II)^6 in the consecutive numbering, we find him to be the second child of 105 (V)^5, Robert; following backward still further, we find 105 (V)^5 to be the fifth child of 60 (I) John Jr.^{4}; who is found to be the first child of 32 (I) John^3, and he in turn is found to be the first child of 2 (II)^2 Samuel; who is the second child of John^1, the original settler in Rhode Island.

MARIA E. (MAXON) TIFFT.

CONTENTS

RECORD OF THE DESCENDANTS OF JOHN TEFFT, of Portsmouth, R. I.

William Teffe, Boston.

It appears by the Town Records, that William Teffe, tailor, "was admitted to inhabit 24, December, 1638," and to buy the house of Jacob Wilson Sawyer, which was sold him the same day.

William Teffe and wife joined the church August 2, 1640.

Perhaps William Teffe's daughter, Lydia, married John Dibble or Deeble of Boston, and had a son Abraham.

Will of William Teffe, of Boston, 1646.

"The first day of the third Month, one thousand six hundred and forty-six, I William Teffe of Boston, in the Massachusetts Bay, doe make this my last Will and Testament. First, I give vnto my daughter Lydia, the summe of twenty pounds, partly, for the discharge of seaven pounds which I received for her in England being a Lagacie given unto her by one Robert Elvinge, deceased, and partly as a Legacie from (myselfe,) so as shee never make other demands of the said Legacie given by said Robert Elvinge, and so she doe not marry without her mother-in-lawe's Consent, or the consent of such friends as her said Mother shall leave her vnto. To be payed in fours of the youngest Cattle, at due prices except the least of all, and in such of the household goods and mon(ies) as indifferently shall reach to the making up thereof according to the proportion of it, (excepting the feather-bed whereon I now lye and vppon the praisement of the goods within two months after my decease, her said portion to be putt forth for her best advantage vntil her age of twenty years or day of marryage with consent as aforesaid, (if shee shall live therevnto, even either of them.)

Itm. I give my least Steere Calfe vnto the Eldest child of my brother John Teffe, to be delivered vppon demand, after my decease, if it be then living, paying for the charge of the keeping of it after my decease vntil it be demanded. All the rest of my goods and chattells, whatvoever, together with my dwelling house and garden and grounds vnder and about it, and all the buildings therevppon, and fences about them, and also together with my land at Long Island, and the barne and fruites growing vppon the said ground both vnder my house and at Long Island, I give and bequeath vnto my beloved wife Anne Teffe, whom I make sole Executrix of this my last will, to her and to her heires and Assignes, forever, and in testimonial thereof I have herevnto sett and putt my hand." WILLIAM TEFFE.

In presence of Tho. Leverett, John Harrison, John Ingolsby.

Testified before the Governour (Mr. No)well, and Mr. Hibbins, by Mr. Tho. Leverett and John Harrison. 2 (9) 1648. Copiavera.

Mass. Archives. Vol. 15 B. p. 69. (This will is recorded at Suffolk Probate office, Lib. VII, fol. 266.) That record contains also the deposition of John Harrison on June 19, 1661, and of John Ingolsby, November 23, 1672, each in regard to an interlineation made in the latter part of the above will.

The said will was Entered and Recorded November 23, 1672. twenty-four years after the instrument was proved.

Record of descendants of John Tefft, of Portsmouth, R. I.

John Tefft,[1] brother of William Tefft of Boston, Mass., married Mary ———, and lived in Portsmouth, Kingstown, R. I. John Tefft died in 1676. Mary Tefft died in 1679.

CHILDREN OF JOHN AND MARY TEFFT.

I. ———.[2]

II. **Samuel,**[2] born, 1644 in Providence, R. I.

III. **Joshua.**[2]

IV. **Tabitha,**[2] born, 1653.

Facts concerning (I) John[1] Tefft.

The first account of him is a freeman in 1655. The freeman (in Anglo-Saxon times) was strictly the freeholder and as a free member of the community to which he belonged, became inseparable from the possession of his "holding" in it. It was this sharing in common land which marked off the freeman from the unfree man, the tiller of land which another owned.

Rhode Island required a freehold estate of $134, for suffrage, and permitted the eldest son of said estate to vote.

1662, Nov. 22. He and wife Mary sold seven acres to Robert Shink of Newport.

1671, May. Kingstown. His name was recorded as an inhabitant of Pettaquamscott.

1674, Nov. 30. Will—Ex. son-in-law Samuel Wilson. To Samuel Wilson, my now dwelling house and 20 acres in Pettaquamscott. To wife Mary, all cattle, viz: two oxen, two cows, two yearling steers, eight swine kind, a ewe and a lamb, and all other movables. To son Samuel Tifft, 2s. To son Joshua, 1s, To daughter Tabitha Tefft, 1s. and an iron pot after wife's decease. Debts to the sum of £1, 3s. to be paid equally by son-in-law Samuel Wilson and son Joshua Tift.

1676, Jan. 26. The death of John[1] is alluded to in a letter from Captain James Oliver, (written at the house of Richard Smith in Narragansett). He first mentions that Joshua Tefft son of John[1] had married a Wampanoag. That he shot twenty times at the English in the Narragansett fight; was captured and executed at Providence, and then declared that he was a "sad wretch, who had never heard a sermon but once these fourteen years," and that "his father going to recall him, lost his head and lies unburied. (See 4 (III) Joshua,[2] son of John.[1]

1679, Nov. 19. His widow signed in satisfaction of her thirds, her signature being witnessed by Tabitha Gardner.

---

2 (I) —— Tefft,[2] daughter of John.[1]

—— Tefft[2] married Samuel Wilson, who was born in 1622 and died in 1682.

CHILDREN OF —— TEFFT AND SAMUEL WILSON.

6 I. **Samuel,**[3]
7 II. **Mary,**[3] born 1663.
8 III. **Sarah,**[3] born 1666.
9 IV. **James,**[3] born 1673.
10 V. **Jeremiah,**[3] born 1674.

Facts concerning Samuel Wilson.

June 21, 1670. Samuel Wilson had a letter sent him by the Commissioners of Connecticut, sitting at Wickfield, requesting the delivery of two of their men, detained of Thomas Mumford, they being messengers of Connecticut inoffensively riding on the King's highway. He complied and released the men.

June 30, 1684. An agreement was made by the orphans of Samuel Wilson with consent of Jireh Bull, executor. The eldest brother, Samuel Wilson, was to have three lots adjoining the housing, with said housing, &c., part had of his father-in-law Tefft. The rest of the land was to go equally to the children including Samuel, and so all of them a share. The agreement was signed by Samuel Wilson,Robert Robert and Mary Hannah.

---

6 (I) Samuel,[3] son of —— Tefft[2] and Samuel Wilson.

Samuel Wilson died in Kingstown, R. I., in 1690.

---

7 (II) Mary,[3] daughter of —— Tefft[2] and Samuel Wilson.

Mary Wilson married Robert Hannah, who died in 1706.

Mary Tefft Hannah married a second time, to George Webb, who died in 1735.

Mary T. Webb died in 1737.

CHILDREN OF MARY AND ROBERT HANNAH.

11 I. **Robert.**[4]

12 II. **Mary.**[4]

---

8 (III) Sarah,[3] daughter of —— Tefft[2] and Samuel Wilson.

Sarah Wilson married John Potter, son of Ichabod and Martha (Hazard) Potter.

Sarah Potter died in 1739. John Potter died in 1715.

CHILDREN OF SARAH AND JOHN POTTER.

13 I. **Martha,**[4] born Dec. 20, 1692.

14 II. **John,**[4] born May 20, 1695.

15 III. **Samuel,**[4] born Sep. 2, 1699.

16 IV. **Sarah,**[4] born April 15, 1702.

17 V. **Susanna,**[4] born March 2, 1707.

18 VI. **Samuel,**[4] born July 28, 1715.

---

9 (VI) James,[3] son of —— Tefft[2] and Samuel Wilson.

James Wilson married Alice Sabeere, daughter of Stephen and Deborah (Angell) Sabeere. James Wilson died in 1706.

CHILD OF JAMES AND ALICE WILSON.

19 I. **Samuel.**[4]

---

10 (V) Jeremiah,[3] son of —— Tefft[2] and Samuel Wilson.

Jeremiah Wilson, married Ann Manoxon.

Jeremiah Wilson married a second time, Mary ——

Jeremiah Wilson resided in New Shoreham and South Kingstown, R. I., and died June 2, 1740.

CHILDREN OF JEREMIAH AND ANN WILSON.

20 I. **Mary,**[4] born Sep. 13, 1701.
21 II. **Ann,**[4] born Dec. 7, 1702,
22 III. **Sarah,**[4] born March 5, 1707.

CHILDREN OF JEREMIAH AND MARY WILSON.

23 IV. **Elizabeth,**[4] born
24 V. **Judith.**[4]
25 VI. **Mary,**[4] born Nov. 13, 1721.
26 VII. **Samuel,**[4] born March 23, 1723.
27 VIII. **Jeremiah,**[4] born May 11, 1726.
28 IX. **John,**[4] born May 11, 1726.
29 X. **Joanna,**[4] born 1728.
30 XI. **George,**[4] born Feb. 1730.
31 XII. **Alice,**[4] born June 15, 1733.

---

3 (II) Samuel,[2] son of John.[1]

Samuel Tefft married Elizabeth Jenckes, daughter of Joseph and Esther (Ballard) Jenckes, and sister of Joseph Jenckes, who was Deputy Governor of Rhode Island from 1715 to 1727.

Elizabeth Tefft was born in 1658 and died in 1740.

Samuel Tefft died in 1725.

CHILDREN OF SAMUEL AND ELIZABETH TEFFT.

32 I. **John.**[3]
33 II. **Samuel.**[3]
34 III. **Peter.**[3]
35 IV. **Sarah.**[3]
36 V. **Elizabeth.**[3]

37 VI. **Esther.**[3]

38 VII. **Mary.**[3]

39 VIII. **Tabitha.**[3]

40 IX. **Mercy.**[3]

41 X. **Susanna.**[3]

Facts concerning Samuel Tefft.

1677. Freeman.

1679, May 12. He was fined 20s. for not attending jury.

1679, July 1. Taxes, 3s., 1½d.

1680, March 12. His fine of 20s. for not attending jury of General Court of Trials was remitted by the Assembly, he having had no warning by the General Sergeant.

1687, September 6. Kings Town. Taxed 9s., 4½d.

1709, June 28. He and twenty-six others bought the tract called Swamptown, being part of the vacant lands in Narragansett, ordered sold by the Assembly.

1721, October 29. His wife Elizabeth, in testifying as to what age James Wilson would have been had he lived, calls her own age seventy years, but other evidence makes her not quite so old.

1725, March 16. Will—proved, 1725, December 20. Ex. wife Elizabeth. To son John, 100 acres in South Kingstown. To son Samuel, south half of homestead. To sons John and Samuel, 135 acres in Westerly. To son Joseph, land in Shannock Purchase, Westerly. To wife Elizabeth, dwelling house, barn, orchards, etc., and north half of homestead for life, and then to sons John and Samuel equally, and these two sons, to be at equal charge in maintaining daughter Tabitha Tift, supporting her for life. To daughters Elizabeth Carpenter, Esther Mumford and Mary Newton, each £20, paid by son John. To daughters Mercy Tift and Susanna Crandall, £20 each. To children of Sarah Witter, deceased, £20. To daughter Mercy Teft a further sum of £30. To granddaughter Sarah Witter, £10 at eighteen. To grandson Daniel Tift, son of Peter,

deceased, £20 if he lives in my family till age. To wife Elizabeth, all movables not given away, at her disposal to children.

Inventory, £1,010, 2s. 8d. viz: wearing apparel, £27, 19s., sword, 11 cows, 4 oxen, 2 pairs of steers, 4 yearlings, 5 calves, 121 sheep, 5 mares, 3 horses, 15 swine, hay £40, pewter, 2 linen wheels, 2 spinning wheels, pair of worsted combs, 6 beds, 2 warming pans, pair of wool cards, carpenter's tools, bonds £155, &c., silver £5, 12s., cider £12, cidermill, 22 geese, &c.

1738, July 4. Will—Proved 1740, May 12. Widow Elizabeth. Ex. son John. To son John, 20s. To son Samuel, 20s. To granddaughter Sarah Witter, £5. To daughters Elizabeth Carpenter, Mary Newton, Esther Mumford, Tabitha Teft, Susanna Crandall, and children of daughter Sarah Witter, deceased, rest of estate.

Inventory, £401, 12s.

---

4 (III) Joshua,[2] son of John.[1]

Joshua Tefft married Sarah———. Resided at Kings Town, R.I.

CHILD OF JOSHUA AND SARAH TEFFT.

42 I. **Peter,**[3] born March 14, 1672. Recorded at Warwick, R.I.

Facts concerning Joshua Tefft.

1676, January 14. He was brought in captive to Providence as related in a letter of same date written by Roger Williams to Governor Leveret of Massachusetts: "This night I was requested by Captain Fenner and other officers of our town, to take the examination and confession of an Englishman who hath been with the Indians before and since the fight. His name is Joshua Tift, and he was taken by Captain Fenner this day at an Indian house, half a mile from where Captain Fenner's house (now burned) did stand." He was asked how long he had been with the Narragansetts, and answered twenty-seven days, more or less. In answer to the question how he came amongst them, he said he was at his farm a mile and a half from Puttuck-

quamscot where he hired an Indian to keep his cattle, himself proposing to go to Rhode Island, but the day he prepared to go a party of Indians came and told him he must die. He begged for his life and promised he would be servant to the Sachem for life, and his life was given him as such slave. He was carried to the fort where were eight hundred fighting men. His eight cattle were killed. He said he was in the fort and waited on his master, the Sachem, till he was wounded, of which wound the Sachem died nine days afterward.

1676, January 18. He was executed, his answers obviously, not being satisfactory to the examiners, but it may still be doubted whether much that is related of him by the old chroniclers is more than fable. It was asserted by these that he was of Providence, which was not the fact, though he was captured there, and that he turned Indian and married a squaw, renounced his religion and nation, and fought against the whites. Probably the closing sentence of one of those narrators was considered excellent religion by some of the readers. "As to his religion, he was found as ignorant as a heathen, which no doubt caused the fewer tears to be shed at his funeral."

---

5 (IV) Tabitha,[2] daughter of John.[1]

Tabitha Tifft married George Gardiner, son of George and Herodias (Hicks) Gardiner, Feb. 13, 1670.

Tabitha Gardiner died in 1722.

George Gardiner died in 1724.

CHILDREN OF TABITHA AND GEORGE GARDINER.

43 I. **Joseph.**[3]

44 II. **Nicholas.**[3]

45 III. **Samuel.**[3]

46 IV. **Robert.**[3]

47 V. **John.**[3]

48 VI. **George.**[3]

49 VII. **Hannah.**[3]
50 VIII. **Tabitha.**[3]
51 IX. **Joanna.**[3]

49 (VII) Hannah,[3] daughter of Tabitha.[2]

Hannah Gardiner married Josiah Wescott, son of Jeremiah and Eleanor (England) Wescott.
Josiah Wescott was born in 1675, and died Nov. 11, 1721.
Hannah Wescott died in 1756.

CHILDREN OF HANNAH AND JOSIAH WESCOTT.

52 I. **Nicholas,**[4] born Aug. 27, 1702.
53 II. **Hannah,**[4] born Aug. 11, 1704.
54 III. **Tabitha,**[4] born Dec. 7, 1706.
55 IV. **Josiah,**[4] born March 6, 1709.
56 V. **Nathan,**[4] born March 23, 1711.
57 VI. **Damaris,**[4] born June 12, 1713.
58 VII. **Caleb,**[4] born Dec. 6, 1716.
59 VIII. **Oliver,**[4] born Sep. 5, 1720.

32 (I) John,[3] son of Samuel.[2]

John Tefft married Joanna Sprague, daughter of Jonathan[3] (William,[2] Edward[1]) and Mehitable (Holbrook) Sprague.
Joanna Sprague Tefft died in 1757.
John Tefft died in 1760.
Resided at South Kingstown, R. I.

CHILDREN OF JOHN AND JOANNA TEFFT.

60 I. **John,**[4] born Dec. 4, 1699.
61 II. **Joseph.**[4]
62 III. **Samuel.**[4]
63 IV. **James,**[4] born April 21, 1715 (date from Munsell's chart.)

64 V. **Nathan.**[4]

65 VI. **daughter.**[4]

66 VII. **Mary.**[4]

67 VIII. **Mercy.**[4]

68 IX. **Mehitable.**[4]

69 X. **Tabitha.**[4]

70 XI. **Sarah.**[4]

Facts concerning 32 (I) John.[3]

1703, Jan. 28. He was one of those engaged in Shannock Purchase.

1754, Jan. 5. Will—Codicil, 1757, Dec. 22—proved 1762, Jan. 21. Exs. wife Joanna and son Joseph. To wife, £500. To son John, 120 acres "near about north from place where the old house stood and did belong to my honored father, Samuel Teft, deceased," having already given to John a tract in Richmond and house on said land. To son Joseph, £300 and a shotgun, having already given him a house and land in Richmond. To son Samuel, a gun, having already given him two tracts of land in Richmond. To sons James and Nathan, 5s. each. To six grandchildren, viz: George Webb, John Webb, Margaret Rogers, Elizabeth Sheblin, Mehitable, James and Mary Teft, £150 divided among them. To five daughters, Mary Barber, Mercy Rogers, Mehitable Rogers, Tabitha Teft and Sarah Brown, £750 equally divided. The rest of estate to children, the six grandchildren having an equal part with them. Codicil mentions decease of wife, and the £500 given her he now gives to five daughters. To granddaughters Margaret Rogers, Elizabeth Shilbe, Mehitable, James and Mary Teft, £5 each.

Inventory, £6,148, 16s., 7d., viz: wearing apparel, £55, bonds £3,137, 9s., 7d., coffee mill, warming pan, 19 sheep, gun, horse, 2 cows, swine, 2 pair cards, &c.

33 (II) Samuel,[3] son of Samuel.[2]

Samuel Tefft married Abigail Tennant, daughter of Alexander Tennant.
Abigail was born in 1690 and died in 1758.
Samuel Tefft died in 1760.
Resided at Kingstown, R. I.

CHILDREN OF SAMUEL AND ABIGAIL TEFFT.

71 I. **Samuel,**[4] born Jan. 19, 1712.
72 II. **Daniel,**[4] born June 14, 1714.
73 III. **Stephen,**[4] born Oct. 5, 1716.
74 IV. **Tennant,**[4] born Sept. 29, 1720.
75 V. **Abigail,**[4] born Feb. 14, 1724.
76 VI. **Ebenezer,**[4] born Feb. 14, 1724.

Concerning 33 (II) Samuel Tefft's[3] Will.

1753, Feb. 20, Will—proved 1760, July 14. Ex. son Daniel. To wife Abigail, half of indoor movables, a cow, bay mare, use of best room, &c., while widow. To son Samuel, £10, he having had his portion. To son Stephen, £30. To son Tennant, £30. To son Ebenezer, certain land. To son Daniel, all the rest both real and personal, and the apprentice boy's time.

---

34 (III) Peter,[3] son of Samuel.[2]

Peter Tefft married Mary ———
Peter died in 1725. Resided at Westerly, R. I., and Stonington, Conn.

CHILDREN OF PETER AND MARY TEFFT.

77 I. **Peter,**[4] born Dec. 19, 1699. Recorded at Westerly.
78 II. **Samuel,**[4] born Feb. 24, 1705. Recorded at Westerly.
79 III. **John,**[4] born Dec. 27, 1706. Recorded at Westerly.

80 IV. **Joseph,**[4] born Jan. 6, 1710. Recorded at Westerly.

81 V. **Daniel,**[4] born April 10, 1712. Recorded at Westerly.

82 VI. **Sarah,**[4] born Feb. 14, 1715. Recorded at Westerly.

83 VII. **Jonathan,**[4] born Oct. 18, 1718, Recorded at Stonington, Conn.

---

35 (IV) Sarah,[3] daughter of Samuel.[2]

Sarah Tefft married Ebenezer Witter, son of Josiah and Elizabeth (Wheeler) Witter.

CHILDREN OF SARAH AND EBENEZER WITTER.

84 I. **Sarah.**[4]

85 II. **Mary,**[4] born 1696.

86 III. **Josiah,**[4] born 1698.

87 IV. **Joseph,**[4] born 1698.

---

36 (V) Elizabeth,[3] daughter of Samuel.[2]

Elizabeth Tefft married Solomon Carpenter, who was born in 1678 and died in 1750.

Elizabeth Carpenter died in 1750.

CHILDREN OF ELIZABETH AND SOLOMON CARPENTER.

88 I. **Elizabeth,**[4] born Jan. 4, 1703.

89 II. **Solomon,**[4] born Feb. 26, 17—.

90 III. **Daniel,**[4] born Dec. 23, 1712.

91 IV. **Sarah,**[4] born Aug. 24, 1716.

---

37 (VI) Esther,[3] daughter of Samuel.[2]

Esther Tefft married Thomas Mumford, son of Thomas and Sarah (Sherman) Mumford, who was born in 1658 and died in 1726.

92 I. **John.**[4]

93 II. **Sarah.**[4]

94 III. **Tabitha.**[4]

95 IV. **Esther.**[4]

Facts concerning Thomas Mumford.

Thomas Mumford's first wife, Abigail, was murdered about two weeks previous to May 28, 1707, by a negro slave belonging to him, and the body of the negro having since been found upon the shore of Little Compton, (he having drowned himself as was believed to prevent being taken alive) it was ordered by the Assembly that his head, legs and arms be cut from the body and hung up in some public place near Newport, R. I., and his body to be burned to ashes, that it may be "something of a terror to others from perpetrating of the like barbarity for the future."

---

38 (VII) Mary,[3] daughter of Samuel.[2]

Mary Tefft married ——— Newton.

---

39 (VIII) Tabitha,[3] daughter of Samuel.[2]

Tabitha Tefft, unmarried.

---

40 (IX) Mercy,[3] daughter of Samuel.[2]

Mercy Tefft, unmarried.

---

41 (X) Susanna,[3] daughter of Samuel.[2]

Susanna Tefft married Peter Crandall, son of John and Elizabeth (Gorton) Crandall.

CHILDREN OF SUSANNA AND PETER CRANDALL.

96 I. **James,**[4] born April 17, 1709.
97 II. **Mary,**[4] born Feb. 17, 1711.
98 III. **Peter,**[4] born July 4, 1713.
99 IV. **John,**[4] born June 18, 1716.
100 V. **Elizabeth,**[4] born Feb. 1, 1719.

---

60 (I) John[4] Jr., son of John.[3]

John Tefft, Jr., was born in Richmond, R. I., Dec. 4, 1699 He married Dec. 11, 1721, at Westerly, by John Babcock, Justice, Mary Reynolds, who was born Feb. 5, 1704.

The Richmond records contain the marriage of John Tefft and Elizabeth James, Dec. 26, 1752.

CHILDREN OF JOHN AND MARY TEFFT.

101 I. **Deliverance,**[5] born Aug. 19, 1722.
102 II. **Sarah,**[5] born April 27, 1725. Died Feb. 1726.
103 III. **Jonathan,**[5] born April 29, 1727.
104 IV. **John,**[5] born March 9, 1729.
105 V. **Robert,**[5] born May 25, 1732.
106 VI. **Mary,**[5] born Sept. 20, 1734.
107 VII. **Patience,**[5] born April 21, 1737.
108 VIII. **Deborah,**[5] born May 18, 1739.
109 IX. **Mehitable,**[5] born Aug. 3, 1742.
110 X. **Elizabeth,**[5] born Feb. 10, 1744.
111 XI. **Jeremiah,**[5] born May 29, 1747.
112 XII. **William,**[5] born Jan. 16, 1749.

The following marriages are copied from the Rhode Island Vital Records, as recorded in Richmond, and it seems probable that they belong to the family of 60 (I) John Jr.[4]

103 (III) Jonathan,[5] son of John Jr.[4]

Jonathan Tefft married Mary Webb, by Samuel Tefft, Justice, Jan. 26, 1794.

---

104 (IV) John Jr.,[5] son of John Jr.[4]

John Tefft married Hannah Clarke, by Thomas Kenyon, Justice, March 14, 1750–1.

---

107 (VII) Patience,[5] daughter of John Jr.[4]

Patience Tefft married Edward Lillibridge, Dec. 4, 1755.

---

110 (X) Elizabeth,[5] daughter of John Jr.[4]

Elizabeth Tefft married Stephen Hoxsie, Oct. 12, 1766.

Will of 60 (I) John, Jr:[4]

In the name of God, Amen. the fourth day of March, 1765, I, John Tefft, of Richmond in Kings County, in the Colony of Rhode Ifland, &c, yeoman, being weak in Body but of perfet Mind and memory, Thanks be given unto God. Therefore, calling to mind the mortality of my Body and Knowing that it is appointed for all men once to Dye, do make and ordain this my laft will and Teftament that is to fay. Principally and firft of all, I Give and Recommend my foul into the Hands of God that Gave it and my Body I recommend to the Earth to be Buried in decent Chriftian Burial at the difcretion of my Executors, nothing doubting but at the General Refurrection I Shall receive the fame again by the Mighty Power of God. And as touching Such Worldly Eftate wherewith it hath pleafed God to blefs me in this Life, I Give demifs and difpofe of the Same in the following Manner and form.

Imprimis I Give and bequeath to my Dearly beloved wife Elizabeth Tefft all her Houfehold Stuff that she had with her before our Marriage and alfo one Hundred pounds old tenor.

Item. I Give and Bequeath to my well beloved Son John Tefft a certain tract of Land Lying and being in Richmond aforefaid and Butted and bounded as followeth, beginning at a Walnut bufh Standing at the Weft End of the Stone Wall Standing on the South Side of the Highway which bufh is marked on three Sides. Thence Southerly with a ftraight line to a ftake and Stones about it. Thence Wefterly to a White oak Tree With Stones about it marked on two fides, all the Lands to ye Weft and North of the before mentioned bounds. Belonging to me to him his heirs and afsigns forever. Item. I give and bequeath to my well beloved Son Jeremiah Tefft all the remaining part of my homeftead farm Which I now live on to him his heirs and afsigns forever and alfo one cow my cart and wheels two fmall draught chains two pair of plow irons and my new horfe chains and collar with my yokes and yoke irons and my old great Chair. . . . . . .

Item. I give and bequeath to my well beloved Son Jonathan Tefft a acertain tract of Land which he now lives on lying and being in the Town of Exeter in ye County and Colony aforefaid all the lands belonging to me on the North Side of the dividing line. Dividing line that now is between him and my Son Robert Tefft to him his heir and afsigns forever.

Item. I give and bequeath to my well beloved Son Robert Tefft to him his heirs and afsigns forever a certain tract of Land that he Now lives on. Lying and being in the Town of Exeter in ye County and Colony aforefaid all the Lands belonging to me on the South Side of ye dividing line that now is between him and my aforefaid Son Jonathan Tefft.

And alfo my Will is that all my Lands Lying in South Kingftown which was given to me by my Honored Father John Tefft in his Laft Will and Teftament to be fold by my Executors and the one half of the money that the faid Lands is Sold for to be Equally divided between my Three Sons, vz. Jonathan Tefft,

John Tefft and Robert Tefft or to their heirs, and the other, half to be divided between my Five Daughters Deliverance Barber, Mary Clark, Deborah James, Elizabeth Tefft, Miriam Tefft and my three grandchildren (to have one) Namely Sarah Lillibridge, Lefter Lillibridge, John Lillibridge to have one equal part of faid money equal to one of my aforefaid daughters to be equally divided between them. And alfo I give and bequeath to my Daughter Elizabeth Tefft one cow Two feather beds and furnature.

I also give and bequeath to my Daughter Miriam Tefft one cow, Two feather beds and furnature and further my will is that my faid Daughter Elizabeth Tefft, Shall have the firft choice of one of the beds and my Daughter Miriam the next choice and Elizabeth the third and the fourth to my Daughter Miriam.—

And all the remainder of my movable Eftate to be divided between my Five Daughters and Three grand Children above Named in the Same manner as is above Exprefsed in the divifion of the money except my corn meat and hay to be for the ufe of my family now under my care, With all the new Cloth belonging to me at my Difceafe. And Further my Will is and I do hereby give and bequeath To my aforefaid son John Tefft the Weft end of my Dwelling House which he now lives in and the Eaft End of my Crib, he removing of faid Houfe and Crib in a Short time off my Land and not to put any perfon or perfons into faid Houfe fo long as it stands on my Land.

And further I alfo give to my afore named fon Jonathan Teflt one beaver hat which I have by me. Alfo I Give and bequeath to my aforefaid Son Jeremiah Tefft my Gun.

And I alfo give and bequeath to my aforenamed Daughter Elizabeth Tefft Tenn Sheep.

Alfo I give and bequeath to my aforenamed Daughter Miriam Tefft Tenn Sheep.

And I do likewife conftitute make and ordain my Two Trufty and well beloved Sons Namely Jonathan Tefft and Robert Tefft my fole Executors of this my Laft Will and Teftament. And I do hereby utterly Difallow Revoke and difannul all and every

other former Teftaments Wills Legacies and Bequefts and Executors by me in any waife before named Willed and Bequeathed Ratifying and confirming this and no other to be my Laft Will and Teftament.

I Witnefs Whereof I have hereunto fet my hand and feal the Day and year firft above written.

Signed, Sealed Publifhed
Pronounced and Declaired
by the faid John Tefft as his Laft Will and Teftament in the prefents of us the fubscribers

JOHN TEFFT [Seal]

WILLIAM BENTLY
The mark of ABIGAIL A. BENTLY
SAMUEL WILBORE

June the 24th day 1767
the above and foregoing
Will was Entered on Record
pr Thomas Lillibridge (Clerk)

True Copy.
Attest H. P. CLARKE
Town Clerk.

---

61 (II) Joseph,[4] son of John.[3]

Joseph Tefft married Esther Brownell, by Rouse Helme, Assistant, Feb. 22, 1729. Recorded in South Kingstown, R. I.

CHILDREN OF JOSEPH AND ESTHER TEFFT.

113 I. **Elizabeth,**[5] born Dec. 20, 1730, in Richmond, R. I.

114 II. **William,**[5] born Feb. 29, 1732, in Richmond, R. I.

115 III. **Joseph,**[5] born March 19, 1737, in Richmond, R. I.

116 IV. **Benjamin,**[5] born June 3, 1741, in Richmond.

117 V. { **Esther,**[5] born Aug. 6, 1743. / **Thomas,**[5] born Nov. 10, 1743. } It is not possible to determine which child belongs to this family.

118 VI. **Sarah,**[5] born Aug. 24, 1747.

119 VII. **Samuel,**[5] born Aug. 29, 1749.

---

114 (II) William,[5] son of Joseph.[4]

William Tefft married Mary Kenyon, by Stephen Richmond, Justice, March 21, 1754. Recorded in Richmond, R. I.

CHILDREN OF WILLIAM AND MARY TEFFT.

120 I. **Hezekiah,**[6] born Dec. 16, 1753.

121 II. **Pardon,**[6] born Jan. 27, 1755.

122 III. **Thankful,**[6] born March 21, 1757.

123 IV. **David,**[6] born April 19, 1760.

124 V. **William,**[6] born March 21, 1763.

125 VI. **Mary,**[6] born March 13, 1766.

---

62 (III) Samuel,[4] son of John.[3]

Samuel Tefft married to Mary Barber, by Rouse Helme, Assistant, Oct. 1, 1727.

---

66 (VII) Mary,[4] daughter of John.[3]

Mary Tefft married to Benjamin Barber, by Rouse Helme, Assistant, Jan. 11, 1729.

CHILD OF MARY AND BENJAMIN BARBER.

126 I. **Lydia.**[5]

---

126 (I) Lydia,[5] daughter of Mary.[4]

Lydia Barber, married Thomas, son of Joseph Tefft, Dec. 10, 1772, by Robert Stanton. It can not be ascertained to what branch Thomas Tefft belonged.

CHILDREN OF LYDIA AND THOMAS TEFFT.

127 I. **Benjamin,**[6] born Sep. 1, 1773.
128 II. **Sarah,**[6] born April 11, 1775.
129 III. **Esther,**[6] born Feb. 18, 1777; died Dec. 1824.
130 IV. **Joseph,**[6] born Apr. 6, 1779.
131 V. **Thomas,**[6] born Feb. 23, 1781.
132 VI. **Abram,**[6] born Jan. 2, 1785; died Oct. 4, 1785.
133 VII. **Lydia,**[6] born Aug. 4, 1786; died Dec. 27, 1786.

127 (I) Benjamin,[6] son of Lydia[5] and Thomas.

Benjamin T. Tefft, married Lucy, daughter of Stephen and Abigail Reynolds, Sept. 8, 1799, by Moses Barber, Justice. Lucy Tefft died Sept. 11, 1811.

CHILDREN OF BENJAMIN AND LUCY TEFFT.

134 I. **Lydia,**[7] born Feb. 3, 1800, in Exeter, R. I.
135 II. **Abigail,**[7] born Feb. 20, 1802, in Exeter.
136 III. **Lucy,**[7] born Apr. 25, 1804, in Exeter.
137 IV. **Rebecca,**[7] born Feb. 15, 1806, in Exeter.
138 V. **Hannah,**[7] born March 25, 1808, in Exeter.
139 VI. **Benjamin B.,**[7] born May 16, 1810.

"The Vital Records of Rhode Island" give the following records of John's marriage, and births of children, as recorded in Westerly.

John[5] (probable) son of 78 (II) Samuel,[4] son of 34 (III) Peter.[3]

John Tefft married Anna Crandall, Dec. 16, 1764, by Joseph Parks, at Westerly, R. I., and his second marriage is recorded as follows:—John, son of Samuel (dec.) and Mrs. Mary Lewis, daughter of Joseph (dec.) married by Elder Stephen Babcock, Nov. 24, 1773, at Westerly.

CHILDREN OF JOHN AND ANNA TEFFT.

Mary,[6] born Aug. 1, 1765.
Nathan,[6] born Feb. 5, 1767.
John,[6] born Sep. 4, 1768.
Samuel,[6] born May 4, 1770.
Lucy,[6] born Feb. 12, 1772.

CHILDREN OF JOHN AND MARY TEFFT.

Joseph,[6] born Oct. 17, 1774.
Peleg,[6] born May 18, 1777.
David,[6] born Apr. 9, 1781.
Lewis,[6] born Nov. 11, 1783.
Fanny,[6] born March 27, 1788.
Annie,[6] born July 9, 1790.

The following is a record of the above John, as given by one of his descendants, Mrs. Rebecca Maria (Tefft) Allyn of Ledyard, Conn.

Mrs. Allyn states that his first wife was a Crandall, and his second wife, Polly Lewis (Polly is an old fashioned nickname for Mary).

The Tefft homestead was built in 1739, and is situated about one mile and a half from the busy part of Westerly, R. I. and is owned by William R. and Walter Frazier, great great grand sons of John Tefft.

CHILDREN OF JOHN AND ——— (CRANDALL) TEFFT.

140 I. John, Jr.[6]
141 II. Polly.[6]
142 III. Lucy.[6]
143 IV. Samuel.[6]
144 V. David.[6]
145 VI. Nathan.[6]

CHILDREN OF JOHN AND POLLY (LEWIS) TEFFT.

146 VII. Fanny.[6]
147 VIII. Nannie.[6]
148 IX. Joseph.[6]
149 X. Peleg,[6] born May 18, 1776.
150 XI. Lewis.[6]
151 XII. Stephen.[6]

140 (I) John, Jr.,[6] son of John.[5]

John Tefft, Jr. returned to the old homestead, in Westerley, R. I., and died, Feb. 4, 1852.

141 (II) Polly,[6] daughter of John.[5]

Polly Tefft married Jarvis Frink.

142 (III) Lucy,[6] daughter of John.[5]

Lucy Tefft married William Fay.

143 (IV) Samuel,[6] son of John.[5]

Samuel Tefft married Nancy ——— and moved to Attleborough, Mass., where he was a gunsmith. He spelled his name Tifft.

146 (VII) Fanny,[6] daughter of John.[5]

Fanny Tefft married David Babcock, April 7, 1808. Recorded in Westerly, R. I.

147 (VIII) Nannie,[6] daughter of John.[5]

Nannie Tefft married Daniel Lamphier.

148 (IX) Joseph,[6] son of John.[5]

Joseph Tefft married Sally Clarke, by Eld. Elkanah Babcock, Jan. 24, 1800 Recorded in Westerly, R. I.

149 (X) Peleg,[6] son of John.[5]

Peleg Tefft married Rebecca Barker, who died June 2, 1843. Peleg married a second time to Sally West,daughter of Simon West, May 12, 1847.

Peleg Tefft died June 2, 1864. Sally West Tefft died May 26, 1880.

CHILDREN OF PELEG AND REBECCA TEFFT.

152 I. **Mary Barker,**[7] born Dec, 10, 1800.
153 II. **John,**[7] born 1804.
154 III. **Peleg Spicer,**[7] born 1808.
155 IV. **Elizabeth B.,**[7] born 1810.
156 V. **Willard,**[7] born 1814.

152 (I) Mary Barker,[7] daughter of Peleg.[6]

Mary Barker Tefft, spinster, died in 1885.

153 (II) John,[7] son of Peleg.[6]

John Tefft married Heturah Barber.

CHILDREN OF JOHN AND HETURAH TEFFT.

157 I. **John O.**[8]
158 II. **Charles William.**[8]
159 III. **Martin Van Buren.**[8]

---

154 (III) Peleg Spicer,[7] son of Peleg.[6]

Peleg Spicer Tefft married Mary Avery, Dec. 7, 1831, who died Aug. 8, 1865. Peleg married a second time to Mercy A. Langworthy, June 30, 1869.

Peleg Spicer Tefft died March 31, 1876.

CHILDREN OF PELEG SPICER JR. AND MARY (AVERY) TEFFT.

160 I. **Peleg Spicer, Jr.,**[8] born Dec. 19, 1832.
161 II. **Jacob Avery,**[8] born July 30, 1835.
162 III. **Rebecca Maria,**[8] born Oct. 18, 1841.

---

160 (I) Peleg Spicer, Jr.,[8] son of Peleg Spicer.[7]

Peleg Spicer Tefft, Jr., married Lydia G. Bliver, Sept. 8, 1856. Lydia G. Tefft was born Dec. 11, 1837.

CHILDREN OF PELEG SPICER JR. AND LYDIA TEFFT.

163 I. **Mary Frances,**[9] born Jan. 16, 1858.
164 II. **Edward Spicer,**[9] born Sep. 16, 1860.
165 III. **Walter Tracy,**[9] born June 15, 1863.
166 IV. **Minnie,**[9] born July 10, 1867.
167 V. **Howard Morton,**[9] born Oct. 14, 1870.
168 VI. **Mabel,**[9] born Feb. 12, 1879.

---

163 (I) Mary Frances,[9] daughter of Peleg Spicer, Jr.[8]

Mary Frances Tefft married Isaac G. Barber, May 1, 1888.

---

164 (II) Edward Spicer,[9] son of Peleg Spicer, Jr.[8]

Edward Spicer Tefft married Clara M. Palmer, Jan. 17, 1881. Clara Palmer Tefft died Dec. 10, 1882.

Edward Spicer married a second time, Florence A Wilson, May 20, 1890.

CHILD OF EDWARD SPICER AND FLORENCE (WILSON) TEFFT.

169 I. **Cornelia.**[10]

---

165 (III) Walter Tracy,[9] son of Peleg Spicer, Jr.[8]

Walter Tracy Tefft married Ella E. Pierce, Nov. 10, 1887.

---

166 (IV) Minnie,[9] daughter of Peleg Spicer, Jr.[8]

Minnie Tefft married Willis J. Standish, Jan. 15, 1889. Willis J. Standish was born Jan. 12, 1862, and died March 19, 1892.

CHILDREN OF MINNIE AND WILLIS J. STANDISH.

170 I. **Fred Harold,**[10] born Nov. 3, 1889; died June 10, 1890.

171 II. **Jessie Marion,**[10] born March 15, 1891.

---

161 (II) Jacob Avery,[8] son of Peleg Spicer.[7]

Jacob Avery Tefft married Martha Ann Rogers, Feb. 4, 1862. Jacob Avery Tefft died Jan. 9, 1892.

CHILDREN OF JACOB AVERY AND ANN ROGERS TEFFT.

172 I. **James Avery,**[9] born July 4, 1864.

173 II. **Hannah Taylor,**[9] born Feb. 21, 1867.

174 III. **Oscar Hoxie,**[9] born June 25, 1869.

---

172 (I) James Avery,[9] son of Jacob Avery.[8]

James Avery Tefft married Hattie E. Wilcox, Dec. 25, 1893.

---

162 (III) Rebecca Maria,[8] daughter of Peleg Spicer.[7]

Rebecca Maria Tefft married Elisha Sattalee Allyn, Oct. 18, 1864. Elisha Sattalee Allyn was born July 10, 1822.

Residence, Ledyard, Conn.

---

155 (IV) Elizabeth,[7] daughter of Peleg.[6]

Elizabeth B. Tefft married Willard R. Frazier.

Elizabeth B. Frazier died Nov. 29, 1856.

CHILDREN OF ELIZABETH AND WILLARD R. FRAZIER.

175 I.[8]

176 II.[8]

177 III.[8]

178 IV.[8]

179 V.[8]

180 VI.[8]

---

181 I. **William R.,**[9] and

182 II. **Walter,**[9] grandsons of Elizabeth Tefft Frazier, and owner of the John Tefft homestead, Westerly, R. I.

---

156 (V) Willard,[7] son of Peleg.[6]

Willard Tefft married Nancy Bliver, Jan. 6, 1846, by Jedediah W. Knight, Justice.

CHILDREN OF WILLARD AND NANCY TEFFT.

183 I. **Annie.**[8]

184 II. **Alonzo.**[8]

105 (V) Robert,[5] son of John, Jr.[4]

Robert Tefft married Abigail Tefft in Richmond, by Stephen Richmond, Justice, March 27, 1754.

Robert Tefft married a second time, Martha Reynolds, of North Kingstown, ——— 24, 1769, by Robert Hall, Justice.

CHILDREN OF ROBERT AND ABIGAIL TEFFT.

185 I. **Abigail,**[6] born Oct. 6, 1755.

186 II. **John,**[6] born Feb. 19, 1758.

187 III. **Robert,**[6] born Feb. 4, 1761.

188 IV. **Joseph,**[6] born Oct. 13, 1763.

189 V. **Patience,**[6] born Dec. 10, 1765.

CHILD OF ROBERT AND MARTHA TEFFT.

190 VI. **Martha,**[6] born May 7, 1771.

John H. Edwards, Probate Clerk of Exeter, R. I., writes Sep. 1, 1894, as follows: "I find no will on record." Sep. 10, 1771. His widow refused to accept administration on his estate, and Jeremiah Tefft was appointed administrator.

---

185 (I) Abigail,[6] daughter of Robert.[5]

Abigail Tefft married Johnson King, and lived and died in Nassau, N. Y.

---

186 (II) John,[6] son of Robert.[5]

John Tefft married Anna Vallett, who was born Feb. 13, 1760. His descendants have no record of his marriage, nor could any be ascertained from the Town Records of Exeter, they having been destroyed by fire in 1870.

John Tefft died in Nassau, N. Y., April 26, 1813.

Anna Vallett Tefft died in Nassau, N. Y., March 23, 1834.

Anna Vallett Tefft's parents were Jeremiah Vallett of North Kingstown, and Anna Bissell, daughter of John Bissell, of North Kingstown. They were married by Immanuel Bishop, Justice.

Wrilson S. Tifft, of Buffalo, N. Y., obtained from the records of Exeter, R. I., the following:

Robert Tefft, eldest son of John and Anna Vallett Tefft, was born March 1, 1779, on the first day of the week. Abigail Tefft, eldest daughter of John and Anna Tefft, was born Oct. 6, 1780, on the sixth day of the week. Jeremiah Tefft,second son of John Tefft and Anna his wife, was born July 23,1782, on the third day of the week. Simon Tefft, third son of John and Anna Tefft his wife, was born on April 27, 1784, on the fourth day of the week. Mary (known as Polly) Tefft, second daughter of John and Anna Tefft, was born June 23, 1786, on the third day of the week. David Tefft, fourth son of John and Anna Tefft his wife, was born July 3, 1788, on the fifth day of the week.

I hereby certify that the above and before written is a true copy of the above names, as appears on and by the records of the Town of Exeter, Jan. 31, 1794.

Witnessed by Stephen Reynolds, Town Clerk.

There were also two other children born to John and Anna Tefft in Exeter, R.I., which was recorded but not witnessed,viz:

Anna Tefft (known as Nancy) was born April 21, 1790, on the third day of the week.

Charity Tefft was born May 19, 1792, on the seventh day of the week.

---

187 (III) Robert, Jr.,[6] son of Robert.[5]

Robert Tefft, Jr., married —— ——. He lived in Stephentown, N. Y., and was buried on the Russell Greeman farm.

---

188 (IV) Joseph,[6] son of Robert.[5]

Joseph Tefft married ———

Joseph Tefft died Jan. 28, 1847, and was buried in the family burial ground, Stephentown, N. Y.

---

189 (V) Patience,[6] daughter of Robert.[5]

Patience Tefft married ——— Finch and lived and died in Nassau, N. Y.

---

190 (VI) Martha, daughter of Robert.[5]

Martha Tefft married Levi Foster, July 8, 1789. Marriage recorded in South Kingstown, R. I.

Deed of 186 (II) John Tifft[6] to Paul Sweet.[5]

To All People to Whom these Presents Shall Come: Know ye, that I, John Tefft of Exeter in the County of Wafhington and State of Rhode Ifland and Providence Plantations, Yeoman, send Greeting:

Know Ye that I the sd. John Tefft for and in confideration of the fum of Two Hundred and Ten Pounds Lawful Silver money, to me in hand Before the Enfealing hereof well & Truly paid by paul Sweet of Eaft Greenwich in the County of Kent and State aforefaid, yeoman, the Receipt Whereof I do hereby acknowledge & myfelf therewith fully fatiffied contented and paid & thereof and of every part & parcel Thereof do Exonerate, acquit and Difcharge him the sd. paul Sweet, his heirs & executors & Adminiftrators forever have given, granted, Bargained, Sold, aliened enfeoffed Convey and Confirmed and By thefe prefents do freely, fully and abfolutely Give, grant, Bargain, Sell, aliene enfeoffe Convey and Confirm unto him the sd. paul Sweet his Heirs and afsigns forever one Certain Tract

or parcel of Land, Situate, Lying & Being in Exeter aforesaid & Contains By Examination one hundred & one acres of Land be the Same more or Lefs & is butted and bounded as followeth: Viz! Beginning at the Southernmoft Corner at a Great heap of Stones in the Corner of the wall then Running Nearly Eaft as the wall now Stands By Land of Benjamin & Martha Slocum to a Stake with ftones Round it, thence Running Nearly South By Land of Benjamin & martha Slocum to a Stake and heap of Stones at John Browning Wall thence, thence Running Nearly Eaft by Land of John Browning to a highway, thence Nearly North By said Highway to the Southeaft Corner of the Land Belonging to Sprague Tefft, thence Running Nearly Weft By Lands Belonging to the Heirs of Jonathan Tefft, Deceaft to a pole in Oliver Spink's wall, thence Running Nearly South By Lands of Oliver Spink to the firft mentioned Bounds so Bounded or Reputed to be Bounded with all the fences, houfes, Buildings, Ways, Waters & Water Courfes, woods & underwoods and all other privileges and Commodities to the Same Belonging or in any Ways appertaining to him the faid paul Sweet his heirs and afsigns forever to his and their only proper use Benefit and Behoof forever & I the faid John Tefft for myself my heirs, Executors and adminiftrators do Covenant, promife and grant to & with the faid paul Sweet his heirs and afsings, that at and Before the Enfealing hereof I am the True Sole and Lawful owner of the above Bargained premifes & am Lawfully Seized and pofsefsed of the Same in my Proper Right as a good perfect abfolute Eftate of Inheritance in fee Simple & have in myfelf Good Right full power and Lawful authority to Grant, Bargain Sell Convey & Confiem faid bargained premifes all But my mother, Martha Potters thirds which fhe has for & during her Life which the faid paul Sweet takes at his own Rifk & I the faid John Tefft do Referve the Buring place that is Now walled in to myfelf for a Buring place for the family of the Teffts to Burry in & that the faid paul Sweet his Heirs and Afsigns fhall from time to time & at all times forever hereafter By force and Virtue of thefe prefents Lawfully, peacefully and quietly, have, hold, use, occupy, pofsefs & Enjoy the Demifed and

Bargained premifes with the appurtenances free & clear & freely and clearly acquitted & difcharged of and from all manner of former or other gifts, grants Bargains, Sails, Leafes mortgages wills Intails, Jointures, dowers, Judgments Executions or Incumbrances of What Name or Nature foever befides my mother's thirds heretofore mentioned that might in any measure or Degree that might obftruct or make Void this prefent deed, furthermore I the faid John Tefft for myfelf my heirs Executors & adminiftrators do Covenant & Engage the above Demifed premifes to him faid paul Sweet his heirs and afsigns againft the Lawful Claims or Demdans of any perfon or perfons Whatfoever forever to Warrant Secure & Defend all But the above mentioned Thirds of my mothers & anna Tefft the wife of the above faid John Tefft for the Confideration above said freely & willingly, give yield up and Surrender all her Right of dower & power of thirds of in & unto the above Bargained premifes unto him the faid paul Sweet his heirs and afsigns forever in Witnefs Whereof we the faid John Tefft & Anna Tefft have hereunto fet our hands and feals this 14 day of January A. D. 1793 & feventeenth year of American Inndependence.

Signed, Sealed & delivered in the prefants of us

STEPHEN REYNOLDS,	JOHN TEFFT,	(Seal.)
SPRAGUE TEFFT,	ANNA (x) TEFFT.	(Seal.)

Wafhington ss. Exeter January the 14 A. D. 1793 their perfonally appeared the within Subfcriber John Tefft Signer and Sealer to the within & Before Written Inftrument acknowledged the fame to Be his own free Voluntary act & Deed hand & Seal thereunto affixed.

Before me,

STEPHEN REYNOLDS, Just. of Peace.

Recorded January the 15, A. D. 1793.

STEPHEN REYNOLDS, T. Clk.

Town Clerk's Office,

Exeter, R. I., Sep. 3, 1884.

I hereby certify the foregoing to be a true copy as appears on record in this office.

Attest:

NATHAN B. LEWIS, Town Clerk.

In August, 1882, and July, 1891, W. S. Tifft of Buffalo, N.Y., visited the old Tifft homestead in Exeter, R. I. He went by way of Wickford, which used to be called Updike New Town, and passed the ten-rod road his father used to talk so much about. It is mostly walled on either side. The country is rough and grown up to second and third growth timber. The farm is stony and unproductive, and is occupied by a Baptist minister 75 years old, who rides four miles on horseback each Sunday, and preaches at two appointments; receiving $2 for his day's services. He had a housekeeper by the name of Tifft. The farm has never been sold for more than John Tifft received for it in 1793.

The family cemetery was found on the farm, but most of the names were defaced by time, there being only a few marble stones. But the names of Jonathan and Sprague Tefft could be read.

The Removal of 186 (II) John Tifft[6] from Exeter, R. I., to Rensselaer Co., N. Y.

Note:—This branch of the family always spelled their name Tifft, after their removal from Rhode Island.

John Tifft, visited Rensselaer County, N.Y., in 1792, purchased a farm, in the town of Nassau, and contracted for the building of a barn thereon. In February, 1793, the family, consisting of John, his wife Anna, and eight children—the oldest fifteen years of age, and the youngest a babe—started for their new home, a distance of 150 miles. The father drove a team of horses, conveying in a large canvas covered sled, his wife and the five youngest children; the household goods were packed in a sled and drawn by two yoke of oxen, and driven by the eldest son, a lad of fifteen: the stock of cows, sheep and swine were driven by the second and third son.

Their route lay through woods much of the way; at one time they were guided by marked trees in a piece of timber called

Beckett's woods. The journey was made in twenty-two days and was accompanied by many inconveniences and discomforts; for, storms overtook them—in one instance a fall of rain and snow, freezing, obliged them to get the oxen and cows shod before they could proceed on their way. If Anna Vallett Tifft, the wife and mother, shrank from these hardships, John, her husband, came to the rescue and inspired her with a portion of his resolute determination; and she, in turn, as the days came and went, reassured her children that they should reach their destination, and there possess—in time—a home with pleasanter surroundings than the old one. We are sure that, in all ways, during that trying time, she strove to exercise that fortitude which became the wife of a pioneer. The older boys, while driving the cows, young cattle and sheep, made the march more a pastime than a hardship. They crossed the Connecticut River, moving northwest, till they reached Pittsfield, near the line between Massachusetts and New York. While crossing the bank of the Connecticut, one of the sleds tipped over. The older boys, Robert, Jeremiah and Simon, had been intrusted with the secret of the place where the money (silver) was stored in a basket and packed in a certain barrel. Anxious for their treasure, they soon assured themselves of its safety, and carefully returned it to its former place. We can imagine the momentary annoyance caused by this mishap; and also the hearty good will exercised in restoring all to rights; and how they again journeyed onward with renewed good cheer and courage. When finally settled in their new home, that eventful journey doubtless furnished the subject of many interesting talks with their neighbors. Even the grandchildren remember the story, heard from their parents, also enjoying its rehearsal.

186 (II) John,[6] son of Robert.[5]

John Tifft married Anna Vallett. See more full account on page 36.

CHILDREN OF JOHN[6] AND ANNA VALLETT TIFFT.

191 I. **Robert,**[7] born in Exeter, R. I., March 1, 1779.

192 II. **Abigail,**[7] born in Exeter, R. I., Oct. 6, 1780.
193 III. **Jeremiah,**[7] born in Exeter, R. I., Jan. 23, 1782.
194 IV. **Simon,**[7] born in Exeter, R. I., April 27, 1784.
195 V. **Polly,**[7] born in Exeter, R. I., June 23, 1786.
196 VI. **David,**[7] born in Exeter, R. I., July 3, 1788.
197 VII. **Nancy,**[7] born in Exeter, R. I., April 21, 1790.
198 VIII. **Charity,**[7] born in Exeter, R. I., May 19, 1792.
199 IX. **John,**[7] born in Nassau, N. Y., July 25, 1795.
200 X. **Sprague,**[7] born in Nassau, N. Y., July 17, 1800.
201 XI. **Joseph,**[7] born in Nassau, N. Y., Nov. 3, 1802.
202 XII. **George Washington,**[7] born in Nassau, N. Y., Jan. 30, 1805.

Robert, Jeremiah, Simon, David, John, Sprague and Joseph Tifft all lived as neighbors in Rensselaer County, N. Y., the farm of each one of them, at some point touching that of one or the other of his brothers.

---

191 (I) Robert,[7] son of John.[6]

Robert Tifft married, Aug. 30, 1801, Anna Woodward, who was born Nov. 3, 1783, in Lebanon Springs, N. Y., and died Sep. 9, 1860, in Stephentown, N. Y.

Robert Tifft was sergeant of a company in Lieut-Col. C. Carr's Regiment, N. Y. Militia, War of 1812, from September 8 to 20, 1814. The regiment started for Sackett's Harbor, N. Y., reached Whitehall when peace was declared, and returned home. He died Dec. 9, 1857, in Stephentown, N. Y.

CHILDREN OF ROBERT AND ANNA WOODWARD TIFFT.

203 I. **Caroline,**[8] born Aug. 4, 1802, in Stephentown, N. Y.; died in infancy.

204 II. **Jonathan G,**[8] born Aug. 28, 1804, in Stephentown, N.Y.

205 III. **Sally Ann,**[8] born Oct. 28, 1806, in Stephentown, N.Y. died (unmarried) Sep. 24, 1852, in Stephentown.

206 IV. **Ulissa,**[8] born April 5, 1808, in Stephentown, N. Y.

207 V. **Caroline,**[8] born Aug. 30, 1809, in Stephentown, N. Y.

208 VI. **Alanson W.,**[8] born July 20, 1811, in Stephentown, N.Y.

209 VII. **Eliza M.,**[8] born Feb. 1, 1813, in Stephentown, N. Y.

210 VIII. **Nancy,**[8] born Dec. 25, 1814, in Stephentown, N. Y.

---

204 (II) Jonathan G.,[8] son of Robert.[7]

Jonathan G. Tifft married Feb. 14, 1824, at the Tucker homestead in North Nassau, N. Y., to Caroline M. Tucker, who was born Aug. 17, 1805.

Jonathan G. Tifft died Jan. 30, 1865, in Charlestown, W. Va.

Caroline M. Tifft died April 12, 1891, in Brooklyn, N. Y.

CHILDREN OF JONATHAN G. AND CAROLINE M. TIFFT.

211 I. **Martha E.,**[9] born Dec. 7, 1825; died July 24, 1827.

212 II. **Jonathan N.,**[9] born June 22, 1828.

213 III. **Henry R.,**[9] born Aug. 20, 1832.

214 IV. **Mindwell A.,**[9] born Sep. 14, 1834.

215 V. **Caroline S.,**[9] born Sep. 3, 1837.

216 VI. **Alanson H.,**[9] born Sep. 18, 1843.

217 VII. **George W.,**[9] born Dec. 2, 1844; died Dec. 13, 1844.

---

212 (II) Jonathan N.,[9] son of Jonathan G.[8]

Jonathan N. Tifft married Dec. 31, 1848, in Illion, N. Y., by Benjamin J. Diefendorf, to Martha E. Fish, who was born Dec. 8, 1827.

Jonathan N. Tifft died March 29, 1883, in Washington, D. C.

CHILDREN OF JONATHAN N. AND MARTHA E. TIFFT.

218 I. **Ada L.,**[10] born Jan. 29, 1857; died March 7, 1857, in New York City.

219 II. **Ella,**[10] born May 17, 1853; died July 24, 1853, in New York City.

220 III. **Etta,**[10] born May 17, 1853; died July 24, 1853, in New York City.

221 IV. **Henry N.,**[10] born Sep. 6, 1854.

222 V. **Herbert G.,**[10] born July 5, 1856; died May 20, 1857, in New York City.

223 VI. **Irving H.,**[10] born Oct. 4, 1858.

224 VII. **William,**[10] born April 17, 1861; died Sep. 12, 1862, in New York City.

---

221 (IV) Henry N.,[10] son of Jonathan N.[9]

Henry N. Tifft married Nov. 20, 1883, in New York City, by Rev. Howard Crosby, to Gertrude Havens.

Henry N. Tifft is a graduate of Columbia College, and is practicing law, and resides in New York City.

CHILDREN OF HENRY N. AND GERTRUDE TIFFT.

225 I. **Gertrude Havens,**[11] born Sept. 24, 1884.

226 II. **Henry Neville,**[11] born July 30, 1889.

---

34 (VI) Irving H.,[10] son of Jonathan N.[9]

Irving H. Tifft is a graduate of Columbia College, is practicing law, and resides in New York City.

---

218 (III) Henry R.,[9] son of Jonathan G.[8]

Henry R. Tifft married Sept. 15, 1859, in New York City by Rev. E. N. Chapin to Mary E. Gray, who was born Dec. 14, 1841. Residence, Brooklyn, N. Y.

CHILD OF HENRY R. AND MARY E. TIFFT.

227 I. **Mary E.,**[10] born Nov. 6, 1860.

---

227 (I) Mary E.[10] daughter of Henry R.[9]

Mary E. Tifft married Sept. 3, 1890, in New York City to Arthur Louis Fay. Residence, London, England.

CHILD OF MARY E. AND ARTHUR LOUIS FAY.

228 I. **Donald Ward Fay,**[11] born July 16, 1894.

---

214 (IV) Mindwell A.,[9] daughter of Jonathan G.[8]

Mindwell A. Tifft married Dec. 29, 1859, in Utica, N. Y., by Rev. S. O. Lincoln to Charles B. Shaw, who was born Feb. 26, 1827, and died Feb. 5, 1876, in Brooklyn, N. Y.

Mindwell A. Shaw married a second time Oct. 8, 1877, in Brooklyn, N. Y., by Rev. H. R. Nye, to George R. Sprague, who was born April 15, 1814, and died May 16, 1889, in Brooklyn, N. Y. Residence, Brooklyn, N. Y.

CHILDREN OF MINDWELL A. AND CHARLES B. SHAW.

229 I. **Lelia C.,**[10] born Dec. 6, 1861; died April 6, 1862, in Brooklyn, N. Y.

230 II. **Charles B.,**[10] born July 10, 1863; died Jan. 4, 1868, in Brooklyn, N. Y.

231 III. **Martha E.,**[10] born Dec. 19, 1866.

232 IV. **Emma L. A.,**[10] born Feb. 14, 1871; died May 28, 1871.

233 V. **Herbert H. M.,**[10] born July 31, 1874; died Feb. 19, 1875.

---

221 III Martha E.,[10] daughter of Mindwell A.[9] and Charles B. Shaw.

Martha E. Shaw married Nov. 3, 1888, in Brooklyn, N. Y., by Rev. J. J. White, to Howard Crocker, who was born June 13, 1865.

CHILDREN OF MARTHA E. AND HOWARD CROCKER.

234 I. **Harveta S.,**[11] born Dec. 11, 1889; died Dec. 11, 1889.

235 II. **Howard S.,**[11] born March 15, 1892.

---

215 (V) Caroline S.,[9] daughter of Jonathan G.[8]

Caroline S. Tifft married Dec. 29, 1859, in Utica, N.Y., by Rev. T. O. Lincoln, to William F. Chittendon, who was born Aug. 12, 1834. Residence, Brooklyn, N. Y.

CHILDREN OF CAROLINE S. AND WILLIAM F. CHITTENDON.

236 I. **William Herbert,**[10] born Sept. 12, 1861, in Brooklyn, N. Y.

237 II. **Henry Neville,**[10] born Oct. 20, 1864, in Brooklyn, N. Y.; died August 6, 1865, in Brooklyn, N. Y.

238 III. **Charles Edward,**[10] born March 20, 1867, in Brooklyn, N. Y.

239 IV. **Frederick,**[10] born Oct. 10, 1869, in Brooklyn, N. Y.; died Oct. 10, 1869, in Brooklyn, N. Y.

240 V. **Esther Tifft,**[10] born Jan. 28, 1872.

241 VI. **Agnes Bertha,**[10] born August 10, 1876.

242 VII. **Helen Hughson,**[10] born Nov. 4, 1878; died Dec. 12, 1891, in Brooklyn, N. Y.

---

236 (I) William Herbert,[10] son of Caroline S.[9]

William Herbert Chittendon married June 7, 1891, in Brooklyn, N. Y., by Rev. C. P. Mains, to Adeline Johnson.

William H. Chittendon died Dec. 13, 1893.

---

238 (III) Charles Edward,[10] son of Caroline S.[9]

Charles E. Chittendon married July 12, 1893, by Dr. Everett, to Lulie Moody Jenkins, who was born October 20, 1868.

---

290 (V) Esther,[10] daughter of Carolinie S.[9]

Esther Chittendon married Oct. 26, 1892, in Brooklyn, N. Y., by Rev. C. P. Rhoades, to Malcom Townsend. Residence, Brooklyn, N. Y.

---

213 (VI) Alanson H.,[9] son of Jonathan C.[8]

Alanson H. Tifft, married Sept. 20, 1865, in Utica, N. Y., by Rev. T. D. Ballou, to Esther R. Underwood, who was born April 8, 1848. Residence, Brooklyn, N. Y.

CHILDREN OF ALANSON H. AND ESTHER R. TIFFT.

243 I. **Kittie,**[10] born June 20, 1868.

244 II. **Mary E.,**[10] born Aug. 12, 1873; died July 18, 1878.

245 III. **Tifft,**[10] born March 15, 1878.

---

240 (I) Kittie,[10] daughter of Alanson H.[9]

Kittie Tifft married June 5, 1888, in Vernon, N. Y., by Rev. Stephen F. Holmes, to Thomas C. Bell, who was born Oct. 23, 1865. Residence, Brooklyn, N. Y.

---

205 (III) Sally Ann,[8] daughter of Robert.[7]

Sally Ann Tifft died Sept. 24, 1852, in Stephentown, N. Y., unmarried.

206 (IV) Ulissa,[8] daughter of Robert.[7]

Ulissa Tifft was married Feb. 24, 1824, in Nassau, N. Y., to John Turner, who was born May 23, 1800, in Nassau, N. Y., and died Jan. 15, 1881, in Veteran, N. Y.

Ulissa Turner died Oct. 1, 1871, in Veteran, N. Y.

CHILDREN OF ULISSA AND JOHN TURNER.

246 I. **Stephen J.,**[9] born May 6, 1827, in Veteran, N. Y.

247 II. **Mary Louisa,**[9] born April 29, 1829, in Veteran, N. Y.; died Oct. 22, 1830, in Veteran, N. Y.

248 III. **Robert Tifft,**[9] born Jan. 28, 1835, in Veteran, N. Y.

249 IV. **Anna Frances,**[9] born Dec. 27, 1837; died Dec. 4, 1890, in Veteran, N. Y.

---

246 (I) Stephen J.,[9] son of Ulissa.[8]

Stephen J. Turner married Nov. 17, 1849, in Veteran, N.Y., by Rev. S. C. Wetherby, to Phebe Jane Hall, who was born May 18, 1826, in Veteran, N. Y.

CHILDREN OF STEPHEN J. AND PHEBE JANE TURNER.

250 I. **Alonzo S.,**[10] born Sept. 2, 1851, in Veteran, N.Y.; died Dec. 4, 1879, in Elmira, N. Y.

251 II. **Julia,**[10] born Dec. 4, 1857, in Veteran, N. Y.

252 III. **John H.,**[10] born May 26, 1860, in Veteran, N. Y.

253 IV. **Robert U.,**[10] born Dec. 24, 1864, in Veteran, N. Y.; died Oct. 12, 1883, in Veteran, N. Y.

---

251 (II) Julia,[10] daughter of Stephen J.[9]

Julia Turner, married Nov. 7, 1883, in Veteran, N. Y., by Rev. O. S. Brown, to Samuel D. Westlake, who was born Jan. 16, 1858, in Horseheads, N. Y. Residence, Veteran, N. Y.

CHILDREN OF JULIA TURNER AND SAMUEL D. WESTLAKE.

254 I. **Robert Turner,**[11] born Sept. 4, 1885, in Horseheads, N.Y.

255 II. **William S.,**[11] born Dec. 30, 1886, in Veteran, N. Y.

256 III. **Helen,**[11] born July 23, 1894, in Veteran, N.Y.

---

252 (III) John H.,[10] son of Stephen J.[9]

John H. Turner, married Sept. 6, 1886, in Veteran, N. Y., by Rev. W. G. Woodruff, to Jennie H. Carpenter, who was born Jan. 25, 1869, in Millport, N. Y. John H. Turner died Sept. 23, 1891, in Elmira, N. Y.

CHILD OF JOHN H. AND JENNIE H. TURNER.

257 I. **John C.,**[11] born July 18, 1887, in Veteran, N. Y.

---

248 (III) Robert Tifft,[9] son of Ulissa.[8]

Robert Tifft Turner married Oct. 14, 1868, at Buffalo, N. Y., by Rev. John Henderson, to Helen E. Boyd, (daughter of General John W. Boyd) who was born Sept. 8, 1845, in Lake Geneva, Wis.

Robert Tifft Turner was graduated from Alfred University and also from Union College, Schenectady, N. Y., in 1861, after which he entered the law office of Hathaway & Woods, in Elmira, N. Y. He has been Mayor of the city of Elmira, and is a public spirited and influential citizen. Residence, Elmira, N.Y.

CHILDREN OF ROBERT T. AND HELEN E. TURNER.

258 I. **Sara,**[10] born Aug. 6, 1869.

259 II. **Wealthea H.,**[10] born May 25, 1872, in Elmira, N. Y.

260 III. **Elizabeth Ulissa,**[10] born Aug. 16, 1876, in Elmira, N.Y.

261 IV. **Samuel G. H.,**[10] born June 18, 1878, in Elmira, N. Y.

262 V. **Robert Tifft, Jr.,**[10] born Aug. 5, 1886, in Elmira, N. Y.

---

258 (I) Sara,[10] daughter of Robert T. Turner.[9]

Sara Turner was graduated from Elmira Seminary in 1890; and married Jan. 21, 1892, in Elmira, N. Y., by Rev. G. H. McKnight, D.D., to H. H. Bickford, who was born Nov. 22, 1864, in Cabot, Vt. Residence, Elmira, N. Y.

CHILD OF SARA AND H. H. BICKFORD.

263 I. **Robert Turner,**[11] born May 9, 1894, in Elmira, N. Y.

---

260 (III) Elizabeth Ulissa,[10] daughter of Robert T.[9]

Elizabeth Ulissa Turner entered Elmira Seminary in 1892.

---

261 (IV) Samuel G. H.,[10] son of Robert T.[9]

Samuel G. H. Turner entered Union College in 1894.

---

207 (V) Caroline,[8] daughter of Robert.[7]

Caroline Tifft, married Dec. 30, 1826, in Stephentown, N. Y., by Varnum Babcock, J. P., to Timothy C. Larkin, who died July 2, 1876, in Nassau, N. Y.

Caroline Tifft Larkin, married a second time August 21, 1881, in Stephentown, N. Y., by Rev. I. B. Coleman, to Charles Wicks, who died Nov. 14, 1885. Residence, Hoag's Corners, N. Y.

---

208 (VI) Alanson W.,[8] son of Robert.[7]

Alanson W. Tifft, married Nov. 24, 1823, in Nassau, N. Y., by Rev. Mr. Hull, to Clarinda J. Tucker, who died in Buffalo, N. Y., October 8, 1859.

Alanson W. Tifft, married a second time, March 20, 1865, in Veteran, N. Y., by Rev. S. C. Wetherby, to Carrie M. Hill, who was born in Adams Center, N.Y., and died Sept. 1, 1875.

Alanson W. Tifft died March 7, 1870, in Mannsville, N. Y.

CHILD OF ALANSON W. TIFFT.

264 I. **Julia A.,**[9] born Sept. 7, 1836, in Holly, N. Y.

---

264 (I) Julia A.,[9] daughter of Alanson W.[8]

Julia A. Tifft, married Aug. 10, 1864, in Buffalo, N.Y., by Rev. L. Stephens, to Job S. Dawley. Residence, Somerville, Mass.

CHILDREN OF JULIA A. AND JOB S. DAWLEY.

265 I. **Harry N.,**[10] born Jan. 18, 1869, in Buflalo, N. Y.

266 II. **William S.,**[10] born Nov. 30, 1871, in Buffalo, N. Y.

---

266 (II) William S.,[10] son of Julia A.[9]

William S. Dawley married Oct. 15, 1893, in Brooklyn, N. Y., to Lilian Beatrice Lapham. Residence, Brooklyn, N. Y.

---

209 (VII) Eliza M.,[8] daughter of Robert.[7]

Eliza M. Tifft, married March 28, 1829, in Stephentown, N. Y., to Lewis Watts Larkin, who was born Feb. 6, 1802, in Nassau, Rens. Co., N. Y.

Eliza Tifft Larkin died in Troy, N. Y., March 14, 1894.

CHILDREN OF ELIZA M. AND LEWIS W. LARKIN.

267 I. **Anna Eliza,**[9] born Feb. 4, 1835, in Stephentown, N. Y.

268 II. **Rosalia Caroline,**[9] born July 30, 1838, in Nassau, N.Y.

269 III. **Lewis Willard,**[9] born June 26, 1841, in Nassau, N. Y.; died April 30, 1884, in Troy, N. Y.

---

267 (I) Anna Eliza,[9] daughter of Eliza M.,[8]

Anna Eliza Larkin, married January 4, 1860, in Troy, N.Y., by Rev. G. C. Baldwin, to William H. Chittendon, who was born in Stephentown, N. Y., April 7, 1835, and died May 6, 1860, in Cleveland, Ohio.

Anna Eliza Chittendon resides in Troy, N. Y.

---

268 (II) Rosalia Caroline,[9] daughter of Eliza M.[8]

Rosalia Caroline Larkin married June 24, 1863, in Troy, N.Y., by Rev. Duncan Kennedy, to Oliver Dexter, who was born July 7, 1840, in Addison, Vt. Residence, Troy, N. Y.

---

269 (III) Lewis Willard,[9] son of Eliza M.[8]

Lewis Willard Larkin, married Oct. 21, 1867, in Lansingburg, N. Y., by Rev. A. B. Whipple, to Teresa Smith, who was born April 15, 1842, in Lansingburg, N. Y. Residence, Troy, N. Y.

CHILDREN OF LEWIS W. AND TERESA LARKIN.

270 I. **Frederick Lewis,**[10] born Dec. 4, 1869; died March 9, 1873, in Troy, N. Y.

271 II. **Lewis Tifft,**[10] born Jan. 26, 1874, in Troy, N.Y.

---

210 (VIII) Nancy,[8] daughter of Robert.[7]

Nancy Tifft, married Nov. 11, 1838, in Stephentown, N. Y., by Rev. I. B. Coleman, to Alonzo Swan.

Nancy Tifft Swan died in Stephentown, N. Y., June 25, 1885.

CHILDREN OF NANCY AND ALONZO SWAN.

272 I. **Nelson A.,**[9] born Nov. 16, 1839, in Nassau, N. Y.

273 II. **Mary F.,**[9] born Dec. 10, 1844, in Nassau, N. Y.

274 III. **Sarah A.,**[9] born Nov. 10, 1853, in Stephentown, N. Y.

272 (I) Nelson A.,[9] son of Nancy.[8]

Nelson A. Swan, married May 1, 1868, in Lansingburg, N. Y., by Rev. Dr. Farrar, to Mary McKeon, who was born in Lansingburg, N. Y.

Nelson A. Swan served during the Civil War under Gen. Burnside, and was honorably discharged at its close. He died May 8, 1876.

CHILD OF NELSON A. AND MARY SWAN.

275 I. **Willis A. Swan,**[10] who is now about 25 years of age.

---

192 (II) Abigail,[7] daughter of John.[6]

Abigail Tifft, married Elijah Gillett. Abigail Tifft Gillett married a second time, Henry Wait.

Abigail T. G. Wait died in Murry, Orleans Co., N. Y., Dec. 28, 1863.

CHILDREN OF ABIGAIL TIFFT AND ELIJAH GILLETT.

276 I. **Nathan,**[8] born June 11, 1797.

277 II. **John,**[8] born Aug. 1, 1805, in Chatham, N. Y.

---

276 (I) Nathan,[8] son of Abigail.[7]

Nathan Gillett, married October 24, 1816, to Betsey North, who was born March 22, 1800. Nathan Gillett died in Hamlin, Monroe Co., N. Y. His wife Betsey may have died in the same place.

CHILDREN OF NATHAN AND BETSEY GILLETT.

278 I. **Elijah,**[9] born Nov. 23, 1817.

279 II. **Abigail J.,**[9] born Nov. 17, 1820, at Westfield, N. Y.

280 III. **Betsey J.,**[9] born July 30, 1822, Albion, N. Y.

281 IV. **Caroline,**[9] born Sept. 30, 1826.

282 V. **John,**[9] born Jan. 20, 1830.

283 VI. **Polly Jane,**[9] born June 22, 1832.
284 VII. **Mary Ann,**[9] born Oct. 26, 1834.

---

278 (I) Elijah,[9] son of Nathan.[8]

Elijah Gillett. Have been unable to ascertain whom he married. Elijah and wife died in Oswego, N. Y. They had three girls and two boys, of whom all are dead except John Gillett.

CHILDREN OF ELIJAH GILLETT AND ———.

285 I.[10]
286 II.[10]
287 III.[10]
288 IV.[10]
289 V.[10]
290 VI. **John,**[10] born Aug. 24, 1853, in Oswego, N. Y.

---

290 (VI) John,[10] son of Elijah.[9]

John Gillett, married in Oswego, N. Y., July 9, 1881, by Rev. William Blair, to Annie Lytle, who was born in Morley, N.Y. in 1857, and died in Oswego in 1895. Residence, Oswego, N. Y.

CHILDREN OF JOHN AND ANNIE GILLETT.

291 I. **Eva May,**[11] born Aug., 1885, in Oswego, N. Y.
292 II. **John,**[11] born July, 1886, in Oswego, N. Y.

---

279 (II) Abigail J.,[9] daughter of Nathan.[8]

Abigail J. Gillett, married Nov. 7, 1841, in Hastings, Oswego Co., N. Y., to Samuel Brown, who was born in Middlefield, N.Y., Feb. 25, 1805.

Abigail Brown died April 2, 1876, in Albion, N. Y.
Samuel Brown died March 16, 1853, in Clarkson, N. Y.

293 I. **Helen E.,**[10] born Dec. 1, 1842, in Mexico, N. Y.
294 II. **James H.,**[10] born Aug. 25, 1844.
295 III. **Anna E.,**[10] born May 24, 1846, in Barre, Orleans Co., N.Y.
296 IV. **Frank,**[10] born Sept. 12, 1848, in Clarkson, Monroe Co.
297 V. **George A.,**[10] born Jan. 21, 1857, in Clarkson, N. Y.

---

293 (I) Helen E.,[10] daughter of Abigail J.,[9]

Helen E. Brown, married July 3, 1862, to Robert Liddle, who was born Dec. 15, 1838, in Schoharie Co., N. Y.

CHILDREN OF HELEN E. AND ROBERT LIDDLE.

298 I. **Anna.**[11]
299 II. **Jennet.**[11]
300 III. **John,**[11] said to live in Carlton, N. Y.

---

294 (II) James H.,[10] son of Abigail J.[9]

James H. Brown, married Dec. 28, 1889, in Ionia, Mich., by Rev. J. J. Phelps, to Mrs. Mary E. Brown, who was born in Schenectady, N. Y., Jan. 27, 1839.

James H. Brown enlisted in Company K., New York Artillery, Col. Porter's Regiment, Aug. 18, 1862, was mustered out June, 1865. Residence, Ionia, Mich.

---

295 (III) Anna E.,[10] daughter of Abigail J.[9]

Anna E. Brown, married Alvin Kenyon. (Separated).

---

296 (IV) Frank,[10] son of Abigail J.[9]

Frank Brown, married Feb. 19, 1868, at Gaines, Orleans Co., N. Y., to Ella C. Curtis, who was born in Carlton, N. Y. Residence, Toledo, Ohio.

CHILDREN OF FRANK AND ELLA BROWN.

301 I. **Cora,**[11] born May 23, 1870.
302 II. **Gretchen G.,**[11] born June 4, 1877, in Swanton, Ohio.

---

301 (I) Cora,[11] daughter of Frank.[10]

Cora Brown, married July 20, 1895, at Toledo, Ohio.

---

297 (V) George A.,[10] son of Abigail J.[9]

George A. Brown married and has five boys. Residence, Brockport, N. Y.

CHILDREN OF GEORGE A. AND ——— BROWN.

303 I.[11]
304 II.[11]
305 III.[11]
306 IV.[11]
307 V.[11]

---

280 (III) Betsey J.,[9] daughter of Nathan.[8]

Betsey J. Gillett, married Jan. 15, 1848, at George W. Tifft's, Buffalo, N. Y., by Rev. Dr. J. C. Lord, to Franklin Brown, who was born in Albion, N. Y., May 14, 1819.

Betsey J. Brown died in Carlton Station, N. Y., May 19, 1878.

Franklin Brown resides in Carlton Station, N. Y.

---

281 (IV) Caroline,[9] daughter of Nathan.[8]

Caroline Gillett, married James Williams, and lived and died in Texas.

Caroline and James Williams had two girls and three boys, grown up, married, and supposed to live South.

CHILDREN OF CAROLINE AND JAMES WILLIAMS.

308 I.[10]
309 II.[10]
310 III.[10]
311 IV.[10]
312 V.[10]

---

282 (V) John,[9] son of Nathan.[8]

John Gillett, married Aug. 12, 1854, in Sweden, N. Y., to Louisa E. Clark of Clarkson, N. Y.
John Gillett died Dec. 27, 1879.
Louisa Gillett died April 9, 1862.

CHILDREN OF JOHN AND LOUISA GILLETT.

313 I. **Clark C.**,[10] born March 6, 1857, in Albion, N. Y.
314 II. **James**,[10] born April 1, 1862, in Hamlin, N. Y.; died Oct. 1862, in Hamlin, N. Y.

---

313 (I) Clark C.,[10] son of John.[9]

Clark C. Gillett, married Nov. 6, 1878, at Sweden, N. Y., by Rev. M. C. Dean, to Annie M. Sargent.
Residence, Morton, N. Y.

CHILD OF CLARK C. AND ANNIE M. GILLETT.

315 I. **Ira H.**,[11] born Jan. 5, 1880, in Kendall, N. Y.; died April 26, 1893, in Kendall, N. Y.

---

283 (VI) Polly Jane,[9] daughter of Nathan.[8]

Polly Jane Gillett married Seymour Sholes.
Polly Jane Gillett died in La Cross, Wis.

CHILDREN OF POLLY JANE AND SEYMOUR SHOLES.

316 I. **George.**[10]
317 II. **Denny.**[10]
318 III. **Frank.**[10]

The above children are supposed to be living in La Cross, Wis.

284 (VII) Mary Ann,[9] daughter of Nathan.[8]

Mary Ann Gillett, never married, and died in Albion, N. Y., Sept. 26, 1850.

277 (II) John Tifft,[8] son of Abigail.[7]

John Tifft Gillett, married Nov. 19, 1831, by Esq. Webster, to ——————— who was born in Trenton, N. Y., July 15, 1810.

John Tifft Gillett died in Murry, N. Y., April 20, 1867.

CHILDREN OF JOHN TIFFT GILLETT AND WIFE.

319 I. **Elijah W.,**[9] born Oct. 27, 1832, in Westfield, N. Y.
320 II. **Henry Gillett,**[9] born Jan 19, 1835, in Westfield, N. Y.
321 III. **Joel,**[9] born Jan. 12, 1837, in Kendall, N. Y.
322 IV. **Daniel,**[9] born May 10, 1839, in Kendall, N. Y.
323 V. **John Tifft, Jr.,**[9] born June 9, 1842, in Bennington, N.Y.
324 VI. **Ellen A.,**[9] born Nov. 12, 1847.

319 (I) Elijah W.,[9] son of John Tifft.[8]

Elijah W. Gillett never married.

320 (II) Henry,[9] son of John Tifft.[8]

Henry Gillett, married by Rev. Chesbow. Residence, Harlan, Shelby Co., Iowa.

---

321 (III) Joel,[9] son of John Tifft.[8]

Joel Gillett died Aug. 26, 1860, at Greenfield, Mo.

---

322 (IV) Daniel,[9] son of John Tifft.[8]

Daniel Gillett, married in Murry, N. Y., by Rev. O. A. Spring.

---

323 (V) John Tifft, Jr.,[9] son of John Tifft.[8]

John Tifft Gillett, Jr., married Jan. 17, 1878, at Council Bluffs, Iowa, by T. H. Cleland, to Sarah Stoker. Residence, Avoca, Iowa.

---

324 (VI) Ellen A.,[9] daughter of John Tifft.[8]

Ellen A. Gillett, married Dec. 30, 1873, at Avoca, Iowa, to Abram Van Zandt, who was born at Carlton, N. Y., April 25, 1837.

Abram Van Zandt's mother was a cousin of General Butterfield. Abram Van Zandt enlisted August, 1862, at Albion, N. Y. as an Independent Sharpshooter under Captain Hezekiah Bowen of Medina, N. Y. Soon after was attached to Company A. 151st Regiment N. Y. Volunteers. Was all through western parts of Maryland and Virginia, where he was severely wounded while in line of duty, and sent to hospital, from whence he was sent to Fort Wood, Bedloes Island, New York Harbor. He was here employed in carrying dispatches between the Island and the city. Remained in that position until mustered out July 4, 1865. Residence, West Kendall, N. Y.

CHILD OF ELLEN A. AND ABRAM VAN ZANDT.

325 I. **William John Paul,**[10] born June 22, 1875, in Fairview, Ia. Residence, West Kendall, N. Y.

193 (III) Jeremiah,[7] son of John.[6]

Jeremiah Tifft, married Jan. 4, 1806, to Mary Brainard, who was born April 29, 1788.

Jeremiah Tifft was Corporal of a company in Lieut.-Col. C. Carr's Regiment, N. Y. Militia, War of 1812, from Sept. 8 to 20, 1814. The regiment started for Sackett's Harbor, N. Y., reached Whitehall, when peace was declared, and they returned home. He died May 23, 1873, in Nassau, N. Y.

CHILDREN OF JEREMIAH AND MARY B. TIFFT.

326 I. **David Brainard,**[8] born Sept. 7, 1809, in Nassau, N.Y.
327 II. **Jeremiah Vallett,**[8] born Nov. 23, 1811, in Nassau, N.Y.
328 III. **Rachel Maria,**[8] born Oct. 30, 1813, in Nassau, N. Y.
329 IV. **Nathan Gillett,**[8] born Sept. 14, 1815, in Nassau, N.Y.
330 V. **Polly Ann,**[8] born May 16, 1819, in Nassau, N. Y.; died April 2, 1841, in Nassau, N. Y.
331 VI. **Amasa Edgar,**[8] born Feb. 11, 1823, in Nassau, N. Y.
332 VII. **Joseph Norman,**[8] born April 22, 1825, in Nassau, N.Y.
333 VIII. **Dorothy Elizabeth,**[8] born May 25, 1827, in Nassau, N. Y.
334 IX. **Emily Sophronia,**[8] born Nov. 8, 1829, in Nassau, N.Y.

326 (I) David Brainard,[8] son of Jeremiah.[7]

David Brainard Tifft, married July 4, 1856, in North Chatham, N. Y., by Rev. William Loomis, to Charlotte M. Wier, who was born Nov. 28, 1832, in Nassau, N. Y.

David B. Tifft died Feb. 2, 1890, in West Lebanon, N. Y.

CHILDREN OF DAVID B. AND CHARLOTTE M. TIFFT.

335 I. **Estelle C.**,[9] born May 29, 1857, in Nassau, N. Y.; died Feb. 17, 1863, in East Nassau, N. Y.

336 II. **Eulalie A.**,[9] born June 13, 1865, in Nassau, N. Y.

337 III. **Iranellie G.**,[9] born Oct. 4, 1870, in Troy, N. Y.

---

336 (II) Eulalie A.,[9] daughter of David Brainard.[8]

Eulalie A. Tifft, married Feb. 25, 1892, in New Lebanon, N.Y., by Rev. Mr. Sheehan, to M. J. Rogers, who was born Oct. 13, 1859, in New Lebanon.

---

327 (II) Jeremiah Vallett,[8] son of Jeremiah.[7]

Jeremiah Vallett Tifft, married Feb. 24, 1838, in Lebanon, N.Y., by Rev. D. Starkes, to Palmira Turner, who was born Feb. 9, 1821, in Nassau, N. Y.

Jeremiah V. Tifft died June 20, 1888, in Nassau, N. Y.

CHILDREN OF JEREMIAH V. AND PALMIRA TIFFT.

338 I. **Lewis E.**,[9] born June 1, 1843, in Hoag's Corners, N. Y.; died Feb. 21, 1845, in Nassau, N. Y.

339 II. **Nelson V.**,[9] born Feb. 20, 1846, in Nassau, N. Y.

340 III. **William L.**,[9] born March 16, 1848, in Nassau, N. Y.; died March 24, 1856, in Nassau, N. Y.

341 IV. **Helen Maria**,[9] born Nov. 3, 1853, in Nassau, N. Y.

---

339 (II) Nelson V.,[9] son of Jeremiah Vallett.[8]

Nelson V. Tifft, married March 24, 1866, by Rev. J. B. Coleman, to Nancy C. Bateman, who was born Oct. 23, 1847, in West Stephentown, N. Y.

Nelson V. Tifft was a Union soldier during the Civil War, was drafted in 1864 and discharged in 1865. He died July 13, 1894, at Glenville, Schenectady Co., N. Y.

CHILD OF NELSON V. AND NANCY C. TIFFT.

342 I. **Lilian May,**[10] born Nov. 1, 1871, in Clifton Park, N.Y.

---

341 (IV) Helen Maria,[9] daughter of Jeremiah Vallett.[8]

Helen Maria Tifft, married Feb. 15, 1871, in West Stephentown, N. Y., by Rev. I. B. Coleman, to Silas J. Bailey, who was born Sept. 12, 1845, in Hoag's Corners, N. Y.

CHILDREN OF HELEN MARIA AND SILAS J. BAILEY.

343 I. **Irving D.,**[10] born March 27, 1880, in Stephentown, N. Y.
344 II. **Hugh E.,**[10] born May 11, 1885, in Stephentown, N. Y.; died Dec. 11, 1885.
345 III. **Grover S.,**[10] born Sept. 12, 1887, in Stephentown, N. Y.

---

328 (III) Rachel Maria,[8] daughter of Jeremiah.[7]

Rachel Maria Tifft, married Dec. 31, 1836, in Sand Lake, N. Y. to George W. Larkin, who was born March 16, 1808, in Nassau, N. Y., and died Aug. 12, 1884, in Nassau, N. Y.

Rachel Maria Larkin died Sept. 12, 1869, in Nassau, N. Y.

CHILDREN OF RACHEL MARIA AND GEORGE W. LARKIN.

346 I. **Lucena Maria,**[9] born Dec. 19, 1838, in Nassau, N. Y.
347 II. **George Lewis,**[9] born Dec. 20, 1844, in Nassau, N. Y.; died Dec. 25, 1854, in Nassau, N. Y.

---

346 (I) Lucena Maria,[9] daughter of Rachel Maria.[8]

Lucena Maria Larkin, married Jan. 1, 1866, in Nassau, N. Y., by Rev. W. O. Ashley, to James A. Weller, who was born May 13, 1839, in Nassau, N. Y.

CHILDREN OF LUCENA MARIA AND JAMES A. WELLER.

348 I. **J. Howard,**[10] born Aug. 27, 1869, in Nassau, N. Y.

349 II. **Dora E.,**[10] born July 4, 1875, in Nassau, N. Y.

350 III. **Rosa Dexter,**[10] born April 15, 1877, in Nassau, N. Y.; died Jan. 9, 1884, in Nassau, N. Y.

---

348 (I) J. Howard,[10] son of Lucena Maria.[9]

J. Howard Weller, married Oct. 6, 1895, in Green River, N.Y., by David Westover, J. P., to Anna Hopeman, who was born Jan. 15, 1868, in Pine Plains, N. Y.

---

329 (IV) Nathan Gillett,[8] son of Jeremiah.[7]

Nathan Gillett Tifft, married March 5, 1836, in Nassau, N. Y., by Rev. A. H. Miller, to Mary M. Barber, who was born April 7, 1817, in Nassau, N. Y.

CHILDREN OF NATHAN GILLETT AND MARY M. TIFFT.

351 I. **Mary Priscilla,**[9] born July 4, 1836, in Nassau, N. Y.

352 II. **N. Orlando,**[9] born Jan. 17, 1838, in Hancock, Mass.; died July 23, 1848, in Nassau, N. Y.

353 III. **William Mortimer,**[9] born Oct. 21, 1839, in Hancock, Mass.; died Nov. 12, 1847, in Hancock, Mass.

354 IV. **Amasa G.,**[9] born Sept. 5, 1849, in Hancock, Mass.; died April 8, 1856, in Nassau, N. Y.

---

351 (I) Mary Priscilla,[9] daughter of Nathan Gillett.[8]

Mary Priscilla Tifft, married ——— 3, 1864, in Albany, N. Y., by Rev. I. N. Wyckoff, to William Henry Loppy, who was born March 26, 1838, in Troy, N. Y.

William Loppy enlisted in the 10th Mass. Regiment, Company K., June 21, 1861, and was mustered out June 21, 1864. He served as Township Clerk of Vineland, N. J., from 1879 to 1881; was Township Collector of same place from 1881 to 1883; also Justice of Peace from 1881 to 1883, and Postmaster of Vineland, N. J., from 1883 to 1887, and Fire Commissioner from 1887 to 1895.
Residence, Vineland, N. J.

CHILD OF MARY PRISCILLA AND WILLIAM H. LOPPY.

Inez M.,[10] born Nov. 25, 1867, in Vineland, N. J.; died March 18, 1868, in Vineland, N. J.

---

331 (VI) Amasa Edgar,[8] son of Jeremiah.[7]

Amasa Edgar Tifft married Feb. 11, 1857, in Lebanon Springs. N. Y., by Rev. Asahel Bronson, to Chloe Hand, who was born Oct. 9, 1831, in Lebanon Springs, N. Y. Chloe Hand Tifft is the daughter of Ira Hand, Esq., who was born in New Lebanon, May 31, 1799, and Martha R. Rose, who was born in Stephentown, N. Y., Feb. 6, 1803. Mr. Hand served his town as Justice of Peace twenty consecutive years, and later as Supervisor for four years.

Amasa E. Tifft spent his early years on his father's farm. Shortly after he was twenty-one, he went to Illinois, where he remained about two years. Upon his return he engaged in business with the Tildens of New Lebanon, N.Y., and soon after settled on a farm near Genoa, Cayuga Co., N. Y., where he lived until his death. As a result of strict attention to farming, united with skillful management, he was abundantly prospered. A few years before his death he built large barns and other out-buildings, with a modern house, furnished with all the improvements found in the dwellings of those living in large towns and cities. The buildings as a whole, are said to be the finest and most convenient in Cayuga County. He was generously helpful in church enterprises, and ready to assist the unfortunate at all

times. He possessed a large share of that indomitable will, so characteristic of the Tiffts, bringing it to bear in all his undertakings. It was said—"In his demise the town loses a good citizen, an accommodating neighbor and friend, and the family a devoted husband and father." He died Nov. 24, 1894, in Genoa, N. Y.

CHILD OF AMASA E. AND CHLOE H. TIFFT.

Edgar Hand,[9] born Sept. 30, 1861, in Genoa, N. Y.

---

356 (I) Edgar Hand,[9] son of Amasa Edgar.[8]

Edgar Hand Tifft married Feb. 1, 1882, in Genoa, N. Y., by Rev. F. H. Gates, to Lizzie Belle Strong, who was born April 7, 1863, in Genoa, N. Y. Residence, Genoa, N. Y.

CHILD OF EDGAR H. AND LIZZIE B. TIFFT.

Ruby Mildred,[10] born October 28, 1889, in Genoa, N. Y.

---

332 (VII) Joseph Norman,[8] son of Jeremiah.[7]

Joseph Norman Tifft, married Oct. 19, 1871, in Buffalo, N. Y., by Rev. J. C. Lord, D. D., to Lily Lord, who was born Nov. 20, 1850, in Pike, N. Y.

Joseph N. Tifft, in his early manhood, exhibited a taste for the legal profession, and read law for a brief period. Abandoning the idea, however, he taught school for a time, and finally went to Buffalo, where he engaged in the iron foundry with the firm of George W. Tifft, Sons & Company, of which he was an active member at the time of his death. He was a man of unusual business capacity, and was universally esteemed for his integrity of character. Possessing a large and liberal nature, he was frank and generous in his dealings. He read much and thoughtfully, few men being better informed on the leading topics of science, literature, invention and art. He was a

Trustee in the Central Presbyterian Church, and a liberal contributor to every Christian and philanthropic enterprise.

He died April 22, 1873, in Buffalo, N. Y., and was buried in Forest Lawn Cemetery in that city.

Mrs. Lily Lord Tifft is the daughter of Harriet Mills and the Rev. Claudius Buchanan Lord, of Marysville, Tennessee. She comes of a long line of clergymen on both sides; and in giving her life to philanthropy and the higher education of women, she maintains the traditions of her family. She is a member of the Board of Directors, and has been since 1881 Secretary of the Buffalo Society for the Prevention of Cruelty to Animals; besides being, for many years, one of the Executive Committee of the American Humane Association, in which capacity she has rendered efficient aid. Mrs. Tifft has also served as a member of the Board of Managers of the Buffalo Orphan Asylum, and acted as Secretary, holding the office for some years. She responded to the call for the organization of the Women's Educational and Industrial Union, becoming a charter member, and is still serving on the Board of Directors, as well as working on the Committee for Protective work. She is also a charter member of the Board of Managers of the Newsboy's and Bootblack's Home, and is interested in the Children's Aid Society. In 1892 Mrs. Tifft was appointed by the Mayor of Buffalo, N.Y. (the first woman to hold the place) on the Board of School Examiners, and was re-appointed for five years, in February, 1895. She was also appointed by Governor Flower in 1894, the only woman on the Board of Managers of the Thomas Indian Orphan Asylum,situated on the Cattaraugus Reservation, N. Y., the only Red Indian Orphan Asylum in the world, and re-appointed for five years in 1895, by Governor Morton. She is Secretary of the National Association for the Advancement of Women, and a vice-President of the Educational Congress held in Chicago in 1893. In November, 1895, Mrs. Tifft was elected Secretary of the N. Y. State Federation of Women's Clubs and Societies. She is also President of the Civic Club of Buffalo,

N. Y., organized in February, 1895, and is a woman of rare culture, ripe experience and good executive ability.

Residence, Buffalo, N. Y.

333 (VIII) Dorothy Elizabeth,[8] daughter of Jeremiah.[7]

Dorothy Elizabeth Tifft (known as Dolly) married Nov. 11, 1876, in Nassau, N. Y., by Rev. I. B. Coleman, to Owen H. Damon, who was born April 28, 1842, in Kinderhook, N. Y.

Residence, Nassau, N. Y.

334 (IX) Emily Sophronia,[8] daughter of Jeremiah.[7]

Emily Sophronia Tifft married July 12, 1856, in North Chatham, N. Y., by Rev. W. I. Loomis, to Adoniram Waterbury, who was born Aug. 28, 1833, in Nassau.

Emily S. Waterbury died July 16, 1888, in Petersburg, N. Y.

Rev. Adoniram Waterbury was converted, and became a member of the East Nassau Baptist Church in 1849. He was licensed to preach by the Second Baptist Church of North Nassau, in 1853. A part of 1854-55 was spent in Michigan doing pioneer work. Returning to his native state, he was ordained by the Petersburg, N. Y. Church in October, 1859, in the service of which church he labored thirteen years and six months. He was then called to the pastorate of the Baptist Church in Lebanon Springs, N.Y., where he labored four years. He afterward served the Greenbush, N. Y. church nearly six years and six months, the Rensselaerville, N. Y. church seven and one-half years, and the Franklin, N. Y. church two years. The next two years was spent in Colorado, where he assisted pastors in extra service, and is now (August, 1895) serving his third year with the church in Tawas City, Mich. He has endeared himself to many who were his co-workers in the churches, and the memory of that work is still cherished;

their hearts growing tender as they recall his faithful, forcible manner of presenting the Word of Life to his listeners.

---

194 (IV) Simon,[7] son of John.[6]

Simon Tifft and Ann Webster (who was born June 3, 1788), were married at the Webster Homestead in Stephentown, N. Y., Esq. Thomas of Stephentown, performing the ceremony. It is remembered that he said: "They are the handsomest couple I ever married." Diligent search has been made to find the record of the marriage, but without success.

Simon Tifft was Captain of a Company in Lieut.-Col. C. Carr's Regiment, N. Y. Militia, War of 1812, from Sept. 8 to 20, 1814. The regiment started for Sackett's Harbor, N. Y.; reached Whitehall when peace was declared, and they returned home. He was also Captain of the Militia of Stephentown and Nassau, N. Y. for a number of years.

Ann Webster Tifft died Sept. 14, 1859.

Simon Tifft died March 3, 1873.

Outline of Ann Webster's descent.

Ann Webster was a lineal descendant of Governor John Webster,[1] who came from Warwickshire, Eng., about 1630-33, and settled at Newton, (now Cambridge) Mass. He removed with Rev. Thomas Hooker's party or soon after, across country to Hartford, Conn., and became one of the original settlers of that city, and one of the founders of the Republic of Connecticut. He was Magistrate (or Judge) from 1639 to 1655, when he became Deputy Governor, and in 1656 Governor of the State (or Colony) of Connecticut. He removed from Hartford, Conn., to Hadley, Mass., in 1659; bought a large tract of land on the Connecticut River, and was again made Magistrate (or Judge) in 1660. Gov. John Webster died April 5, 1661, at Hadley, Mass., where he was buried. His grave was not marked until his descendant, Noah Webster, of Dictionary fame, had a tombstone erected over it. His wife's first name was Agnes.

Nothing more is known of her, and it is not known whether he married her in England or in this country. Agnes died in 1667.

One of his four sons was Thomas.[2] It is not known when he was born, or whether he was born in this country. He married at Northampton, Mass., June 16, 1663, Abigail Alexander of Northampton. Thomas and one other son went to Hadley with Governor John, the other son remained in Connecticut.

Thomas Webster died at Northfield, Mass., in 1686, and his wife died there before 1690.

One of the two sons of Thomas Webster[2] was George,[3] who was born at Northampton, Nov. 7, 1670, and was married there in 1696 to Sarah Bliss of Springfield, Mass. He was one of the original settlers and founders of the town of Lebanon, Conn. Land was "set off" to him in that town in 1699. He died there April 12, 1721, and his wife died in 1759 or 1760.

One of the sons of George Webster[3] was Pelatiah,[4] who was born at Lebanon, Nov. 17, 1702, and who married at Lebanon, Dec. 14, 1725, Joanna Smith.

Pelatiah Webster died at Lebanon, Feb. 15, 1756, and his widow died there prior to 1771.

One of Pelatiah's[4] sons was Constant,[5] who was born at Lebanon, Dec. 7, 1741, and married between 1755 and 1760 Miss Kinnie (or Miss Wordsworth,—his descendants do not agree on the name, and no record can be found), for his first wife. He was bound out at the age of about fourteen years, to a neighbor, to learn the blacksmith trade, but ran away soon and enlisted in the French and Indian Wars of 1755-63. There is record of service rendered by him in Capt. A. Fitch's Co., 2nd Conn. Regiment, from April 13 to Dec. 4, 1761, 33 weeks and 5 days, for which he was paid £16, 17s., 1d. His company was mustered out in June, 1761, at Albany, N. Y.

Constant Webster[5] settled at Worthington, Mass., where he owned a farm and carried on his trade as a blacksmith. He was captain of a militia Company there and a member of the Congregational church. He died in Worthington, Mass., about 1826. The date of death of his first wife is not known.

Constant[5] had a brother, Pelatiah Webster, who was a noted political writer at the time of the Revolutionary War. A brief account of him will be found in "Drake's Dictionary of American Biography," also in "Hinman's Connecticut in the Revolution."

One of Constant's[5] children by his first wife was Constant, Jr.,[6] who was born about 1760, and who married at Worthington, Mass., about 1787, Chloe Daniel (born Jan. 19, 1766, daughter of Walter Daniel). He was a blacksmith and farmer. He died at Stephentown, Rensselaer Co., N.Y., Feb. 1830. It is not known when his wife died. He was the father of Mrs. Ann (Webster) Tifft.[7]

CHILDREN OF SIMON AND ANN W. TIFFT.

358 I. **Elijah Gillett,**[8] born July 10, 1809, in Nassau, N. Y.

359 II. **Hamilton Webster,**[8] born June 20, 1811, in Nassau, N. Y.

360 III. **Chloe Ann,**[8] born Aug. 19, 1813, in Nassau, N. Y.

361 IV. **John,**[8] born May 18, 1815, in Nassau, N. Y.

362 V. **Mary,**[8] born March 25, 1817, in Nassau, N. Y.

363 VI. **Abby G. W.,**[8] born Oct. 10, 1819, in Nassau, N. Y.

364 VII. **Sophia,**[8] born May 29, 1822, in Nassau, N, Y.; died Sept. 20, 1824.

365 VIII. **Wrilson Simon,**[8] born Jan. 10, 1825, in Nassau, N.Y.

366 IX. **Frances Sophia,**[8] born Dec. 23, 1827, in Nassau, N.Y.

367 X. **Webster,**[8] born March 18, 1832, in Nassau, N. Y.; died July 8, 1837, in Nassau, N. Y.

358 (I) Elijah G.,[8] son of Simon.[7]

Elijah Gillett Tifft married March 11, 1831, to Lydia Thomas, who was born June 19, 1811, in Stephentown, N. Y.

Lydia Thomas Tifft died in Hoag's Corners, N. Y.

Elijah Gillett Tifft married a second time, Aug. 29, 1837, to

Lydia Ann Lewis, who was born Oct. 20, 1818, in Nassau, N. Y., and died June 23, 1891, in Titusville, Pa., and was buried in Angola, N. Y.

Elijah Gillett Tifft was a Supervisor of Nassau two terms, Deputy Sheriff of Rensselaer County six or eight years. He was a successful business man, being a merchant of Hoag's Corners and later of Angola, N. Y.
Elijah Gillett Tifft died at Angola, N. Y., April 7, 1883.

CHILDREN OF ELIJAH AND LYDIA THOMAS TIFFT.

368 I. **Ursula,**[9] born May 27, 1831, in Nassau, N. Y.
369 II. **Ann Mary,**[9] born Feb. 12, 1835, in Nassau, N. Y.

CHILDREN OF ELIJAH AND LYDIA ANN TIFFT.

370 III. **Elizabeth,**[9] born July 27, 1838, in Nassau, N. Y.
371 IV. **Simon E.,**[9] born May 27, 1840, in Nassau, N. Y.
372 V. **Eugenia Adelaide,**[9] born May 7, 1843, in Nassau, N. Y.
373 VI. **Eudora J.,**[9] born Dec. 28, 1847, in Nassau, N. Y.
374 VII. **Zachary Taylor,**[9] born March 10, 1850, in Nassau, N. Y.
375 VIII. **Winfield Scott,**[9] born Sept. 28, 1852, in Nassau, N. Y.
376 IX. **Charles L.,**[9] born Feb. 2, 1856, in Angola, N. Y.; died April 10, 1883, in Angola, N. Y.

---

368 (I) Ursula,[9] daughter of Elijah Gillett.[8]

Ursula Tifft, married June 2, 1849, in Sand Lake, N. Y., by Rev. A. Miller, to Levi Moore, who was born Nov. 16, 1827, in Lime Plains, N. Y.
Ursula T. Moore died Nov. 16, 1866, in Stephentown, N. Y.
Levi Moore died May 21, 1894, in Stephentown, N. Y.

CHILDREN OF URSULA TIFFT AND LEVI MOORE.

377 I. **Leonella,**[10] born March 25, 1851, in Pittsfield, Mass.
378 II. **Franklin E.,**[10] born Jan. 21, 1853, in Stephentown, N. Y.

379 III. **Elizabeth,**[10] born Oct. 14, 1854, in Stephentown, N.Y.
380 IV. **Agnes,**[10] born April 5, 1856, in Stephentown, N. Y.; died May 9, 1878, in Stephentown, N. Y.
381 V. **Infant daughter,**[10] born Oct. 18, 1857, in Stephentown, N. Y.; died Nov. 28, 1857, in Stephentown.
382 VI. **Charles L.,**[10] born Nov. 25, 1858, in Stephentown, N.Y.
383 VII. **Stephen A. D.,**[10] born Aug. 11, 1861, in Stephentown, N. Y.
384 VIII. **Harriet,**[10] born March 26, 1864, in Stephentown, N. Y.

---

377 (I) Leonella,[10] daughter of Ursula.[9]

Leonella Moore, married Nov. 15, 1879, in Lebanon Springs, by Rev. E. A. Kendall, to Don Aurelius Gardiner, who was born May 2, 1846, in Hancock, Mass.

Mrs. Gardiner's paternal grandfather was born in Holland, and her paternal grandmother was a Hicks, a lineal descendant of Sir Thomas Hicks, a Scottish nobleman who came to America in the Mayflower, and landed with the Pilgrims at Plymouth Rock.

CHILDREN OF LEONELLA AND D. A. GARDINER.

385 I. **Maude A.,**[11] born May 31, 1881, in Hancock, Mass.
386 II. **Howard J.,**[11] born Sept. 1891, in Hancock, Mass.

---

378 (II) Franklin E.,[10] son of Ursula.[9]

Franklin E. Moore, married April 8, 1894, to Nancy Button. Residence, Illinois.

---

379 (III) Elizabeth,[10] daughter of Ursula.[9]

Elizabeth Moore, married Feb. 22, 1877, in Stephentown, N. Y., by Rev. G. H. Day, to Noah Gardner, who was born Nov. 21, 1854, in Stephentown, N. Y.

Residence, Stephentown, N. Y.

---

382 (VI) Charles L.,[10] son of Ursula.[9]

Charles L. Moore, married March 6, 1880, in Stephentown, by Rev. I. B. Coleman, to Jennie Bradway, who was born Dec. 8, 1861, in Stephentown, N. Y.

Residence, West Union St., Pittsfield, Mass.

CHILDREN OF CHARLES L. AND JENNIE MOORE.

387 I. **Walter,**[11] born Dec. 3, 1880, in Hancock, Mass.

388 II. **Wyatt,**[11] born Dec. 19, 1881, in Hancock, Mass.

389 III. **Clarence C.,**[11] born May 24, 1884, in Pittsfield, Mass.

---

383 (VII) Stephen A. D.,[10] son of Ursula.[9]

Stephen A. D. Moore, married Aug. 11, 1883, in Stephentown, N. Y., by Rev. Mr. Harlow, to Theresa Brockway.

Residence, High St., Pittsfield, Mass.

CHILDREN OF STEPHEN A. D. AND THERESA MOORE.

390 I. **Bessie,**[11] born April 16, 1887, in Pittsfield, Mass.

391 II. **Agnes,**[11] born Jan. 21, 1889, in Pittsfield, Mass.

392 III. **Franklin Albert,**[11] born Oct. 13, 1892, in Pittsfield, Mass.

393 IV. **Adelia Susie,**[11] born March 21, 1894, in Canaan, Conn.

---

384 (VIII) Harriet,[10] daughter of Ursula.[9]

Harriet Moore, married in Malden Bridge, N. Y., to Amos Bills, who was born Oct. 22, 1861, in Charlonvillard, Contont, Hericourt, Haute Saone, France.

Residence, Green River, Col. Co., N. Y.

CHILD OF HARRIET AND AMOS BILLS.

394 I. **Clarence Alexander,**[11] born Aug. 24, 1884, in Green River.

---

369 (II) Ann Mary,[8] daughter of Elijah Gillett.[7]

Ann Mary Tifft, married in Pittsfield, Mass., by Rev. Mr. Cole, to Leander Sterling, who was born March 26, 1829, in Portsmouth, N. H., and died Feb. 2, 1895, in Shawneetown, Ill.

Ann Mary Sterling died Sept. 19, 1876, in Ellicottville, N. Y.

CHILDREN OF ANN MARY AND LEANDER STERLING.

395 I. **Alice Velona,**[9] born June 12, 1853, in Nassau, N. Y.

396 II. **Lewellyn,**[9] born June 16, 1857, in Nassau, N. Y.

397 III. **Blanche Estelle,**[9] born Aug. 11, 1869, in Ellicottville, N. Y.; died April 12, 1890, in Denver, Colo.

---

395 (I) Alice Velona,[9] daughter of Ann Mary.[8]

Alice Velona Sterling, married Oct. 21, 1876, in Ellicottville, N. Y., to Junior Bennett, who was born Jan. 13, 1854, in Ellery Center, N. Y.

Residence, Perry, Mich.

CHILD OF ALICE V. AND JUNIOR BENNETT.

398 I. **Frank B.,**[10] born May 27, 1887, in Locke, Mich.

---

396 (II) Lewellyn,[9] son of Ann Mary.[8]

Lewellyn Sterling, married Dec. 24, 1882, in Hartland, Mich., by Isaac W. Lamb, to Adella De Lancy (divorced).

Lewellyn Sterling has held many local offices, been chairman at conventions,and has been Director of the Implement Dealer's Association of Michigan for several years.

Residence, Stanton, Mich.

CHILD OF LEWELLYN AND ADELLA STERLING.

399 I. **Edna,**[10] born June 30, 1884, in Locke, Mich.

370 (III) Elizabeth,[9] daughter of Elijah Gillett.[8]

Elizabeth Tifft, married Sept. 15, 1859, in Angola, N. Y., to James M. Beman, who was born Feb. 14, 1835, in Attica, N. Y.

Residence, Ottawa, Ill.

CHILD OF ELIZABETH AND JAMES M. BEEMAN.

400 I. **Lewis Tifft,**[10] born April 24, 1864, in Angola, N. Y.

---

371 (IV) Simon E.,[9] son of Elijah Gillett.[8]

Simon E. Tifft, married Sept. 26, 1863, in Evans Center, N.Y., by Rev. William Gould, to Sarah Cecelia Ayer (daughter of Ira and Julia Maria Ayer of Evans Center) who was born Nov. 29, 1842.

Simon E. Tifft graduated from the Business College of Buffalo, N. Y., about 1860. Residence, Titusville, Pa.

CHILDREN OF SIMON E. AND SARAH C. TIFFT.

401 I. **Herbert C.,**[10] born Jan. 15, 1867, in Angola, N. Y.; died Sept. 5, 1867.

402 II. **Simon E., Jr.,**[10] born Aug. 8, 1868, in Angola, N. Y.; died Aug. 23, 1870, in Angola, N. Y.

403 III. **Julia Ayer,**[10] born Aug. 17, 1871, in Titusville, Pa.

404 IV. **Gertrude Elizabeth,**[10] born Aug. 24, 1875, in Titusville, Pa.

---

403 (III) Julia Ayer,[10] daughter of Simon E.[9]

Julia Ayer Tifft graduated from the Titusville High School in 1887, and from Cornell University in 1893 with the degree of Ph. B. Was married June 27, 1895, in Ithaca, N. Y., by Rev. C. M. Tyler, A. M., D. D., (Professor in Cornell University) to Lewis Hutchinson Galbreath, who was born Dec. 22, 1861,

in Ashmore, Ill., and graduated from Cornell University in 1890 with the degree of B. L., and obtained a fellowship. He also took a two years' post-graduate course. Mr. Galbreath has taught Psychology in the Normal school of Winona, Minn., for three years. He read a report of the Minnesota Child Study Association at the National Educational Association Convention in Buffalo, N. Y., June 1896, also gave daily lectures upon Correlation at the Buffalo School of Pedagogy, 1896, and is teacher of Psychology in the Northern Illinois Normal University, at Normal, Ill.

---

404 (IV) Gertrude Elizabeth,[10] daughter of Simon E.[9]

Gertrude Elizabeth Tifft graduated from Titusville High School in 1892, and entered Cornell University, Ph. B. class of 1897.

---

372 (V) Eugenia Adelaide[9], daughter of Elijah Gillett.[8]

Eugenia Adelaide Tifft, married Jan. 21, 1866, in Angola, N.Y., by Rev. S. D. Taylor, to John Martin, who was born Oct. 5, 1837, in Evans, N. Y., and died Dec. 18, 1884, in Los Angeles, Cal., and buried at Angola, N. Y. During the Civil War he was enlisted in Co. C, 116th Regiment N. Y. Volunteers. He was the chief musician of his Regiment. Was mustered Sept 3, 1862, and discharged Jan. 16, 1865. He was a member of Bidwell Wilkenson Post No. 9, G. A. R. Eugenia Tifft Martin married a second time, Jan. 9, 1893, in Buffalo, N. Y., by F. S. Fitch, D. D., to Duane Williams Carrier, who was born Jan. 30, 1837, in Marshall, N. Y.

Residence, Angola, N. Y.

CHILDREN OF EUGENIA A. AND JOHN MARTIN.

405 I. **Jennie Tifft,**[10] born May 29, 1867, in Angola, N. Y.
406 II. **Harry Delos,**[10] born June 2, 1869, in Angola, N. Y.
407 III. **Mary Elizabeth,**[10] born Sept. 2, 1871, in Angola, N.Y.

---

405 (I) Jennie Tifft,[10] daughter of Eugenia Adelaide.[9]

Jennie Tifft Martin is a graduate of Cornell University and was State Secretary of the Y. W. C. A. for Illinois, headquarters at Chicago, 1892-95. Also Field Secretary of the Womans Board of Foreign Missions for the Interior, (Congregational) until obliged to resign on account of ill health. Residence, Buffalo, N. Y.

---

406 (II) Harry Delos,[10] son of Eugenia Adelaide.[9]

Harry Delos Martin is a graduate of the Toronto, Canada, Veterinary College of Surgeons. Residence, Buffalo, N. Y.

---

407 (III) Mary E.,[10] daughter of Eugenia Adelaide.[9]

Mary Elizabeth Martin, married July 11, 1895, in Buffalo, N. Y., by Rev. Frank S. Fitch, D. D., to George Hall Ashley, who was born Aug. 9, 1866, in Rochester, N. Y. He was graduated from Cornell University in 1890, with the degree of M. E., received in 1892 the degree of A. M., and in 1894 Ph. D. from the Stanford University. He is a specialist in geology and taught science in the High School of San Bernardino, Cal., for the year of 1895-96, and is assistant State Geologist of Indiana.

---

373 (VI) Eudora J.,[9] daughter of Elijah Gillett.[8]

Eudora J. Tifft, married December 18, 1867, in Angola, N. Y., by Rev. Charles Strong, to John Herbert Dingman, who was born Dec. 22, 1839, in Evans, N. Y. He enlisted in the 116th Regiment N. Y. S. Volunteers in July, 1862; was commissioned 2nd Lieutenant in August, 1864, and commissioned 1st Lieutenant in Jan. 1865. Mustered out of service June 8, 1865.

Residence, Titusville, Pa.

CHILDREN OF EUDORA J. AND JOHN H. DINGMAN.

I. **Mabel,**[10] born Nov. 25, 1871; died Oct. 9, 1873.

II. **Lewis Ray,**[10] born July 27, 1874, in Titusville, Pa.

---

374 (VII) Zachary Taylor,[9] son of Elijah Gillett.[8]

Zachary Taylor Tifft is a prosperous business man of Titusville, Pa.

---

375 (VIII) Winfield Scott,[9] son of Elijah Gillett.[8]

Winfield Scott Tifft, residence, Angola, N. Y.

---

359 (II) Hamilton Webster,[8] son of Simon.[7]

Hamilton Webster Tifft, married January 2, 1836, in Canaan, N. Y., by the Rev. Mr. Clark, to Lydia Ann Watson, who was born July 6, 1817, in Canaan, N. Y.

Hamilton W. Tifft died March 4, 1883, in East Nassau, N. Y.

Lydia Ann Tifft died Aug. 16, 1887, in East Nassau, N. Y.

CHILDREN OF HAMILTON W. AND LYDIA ANN TIFFT.

I. **William H.,**[9] born Sept. 5, 1836, in Canaan, N. Y.

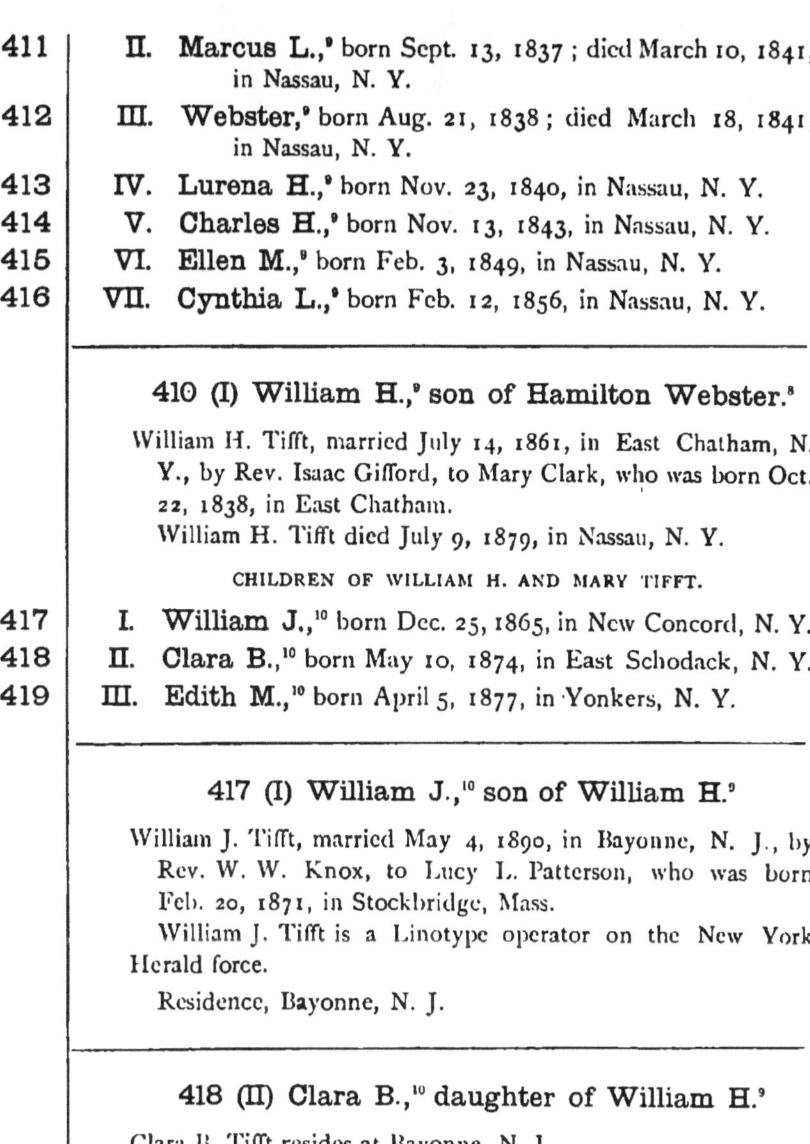

411 II. **Marcus L.,**[9] born Sept. 13, 1837; died March 10, 1841, in Nassau, N. Y.

412 III. **Webster,**[9] born Aug. 21, 1838; died March 18, 1841, in Nassau, N. Y.

413 IV. **Lurena H.,**[9] born Nov. 23, 1840, in Nassau, N. Y.

414 V. **Charles H.,**[9] born Nov. 13, 1843, in Nassau, N. Y.

415 VI. **Ellen M.,**[9] born Feb. 3, 1849, in Nassau, N. Y.

416 VII. **Cynthia L.,**[9] born Feb. 12, 1856, in Nassau, N. Y.

---

410 (I) William H.,[9] son of Hamilton Webster.[8]

William H. Tifft, married July 14, 1861, in East Chatham, N. Y., by Rev. Isaac Gifford, to Mary Clark, who was born Oct. 22, 1838, in East Chatham.

William H. Tifft died July 9, 1879, in Nassau, N. Y.

CHILDREN OF WILLIAM H. AND MARY TIFFT.

417 I. **William J.,**[10] born Dec. 25, 1865, in New Concord, N. Y.

418 II. **Clara B.,**[10] born May 10, 1874, in East Schodack, N. Y.

419 III. **Edith M.,**[10] born April 5, 1877, in Yonkers, N. Y.

---

417 (I) William J.,[10] son of William H.[9]

William J. Tifft, married May 4, 1890, in Bayonne, N. J., by Rev. W. W. Knox, to Lucy L. Patterson, who was born Feb. 20, 1871, in Stockbridge, Mass.

William J. Tifft is a Linotype operator on the New York Herald force.

Residence, Bayonne, N. J.

---

418 (II) Clara B.,[10] daughter of William H.[9]

Clara B. Tifft resides at Bayonne, N. J.

---

416 (III) Edith M.,[10] daughter of William H.[9]

Edith M. Tifft resides at Bayonne, N. J.

---

413 (IV) Lurena H.,[9] daughter of Hamilton Webster.[8]

Lurena H. Tifft, married Feb. 23, 1861, in West Stephentown, N. Y., by Rev. I. B. Coleman, to Dalmar W. Dunham, who was born April 6, 1836, in Nassau, N. Y.

Dalmar W. Dunham enlisted Aug. 6, 1862, in the 125th N. Y. S.V., Company E; was promoted to corporal Aug. 27, 1862, with the highest praise of his Lieutenant, and fell in the battle of Gettysburg July 3, 1863, while honorably discharging his duty. He was removed from the field and buried at Nassau, N. Y.

Lurena H. Dunham married a second time, March 12, 1873, in Yonkers, N. Y., by Rev. Mr. Burr, to Calvin Phillips.

Lurena H. Phillips died May 15, 1874, in Hoag's Corners, N. Y.

Calvin Phillips died Nov. 10, 1874, in Hoag's Corners, N.Y.

---

414 (V) Charles H.,[9] son Hamilton Webster.[8]

Charles H. Tifft, married Dec. 21, 1872, in Portland, Mich., by Rev. L. P. Spelman, to Lavantha C. Dow, who was born May 22, 1847,—in Victory, N. Y.

Residence, Vineland, N. Y.

CHILDREN OF CHARLES H. AND LEVANTHA TIFFT.

420 I. **Minnie Lurena,**[10] born June 22, 1874, in East Nassau, N. Y.

421 II. **C. Arthur,**[10] born April 1, 1878, in Yonkers, N. Y.

420 (I) Minnie Lurena,[10] daughter of Charles H.[9]

Minnie L. Tifft was graduated from the High School in Vineland, N. Y., 1893 and was class poetess.

415 (VI) Ellen M.,[9] daughter of Hamilton Webster.[8]

Ellen M. Tifft, married Oct. 23, 1864, in Chatham, N. Y., by Rev. Mr. Mead, to Alfred Strait, who was born Jan. 12, 1847, in East Nassau, N. Y.

Residence, East Nassau, N. Y.

CHILDREN OF ELLEN M. AND ALFRED STRAIT.

422 I. **Emily E.,**[10] born December 25, 1865, in East Nassau, N. Y.; died Aug. 25, 1868.

423 II. **Carrie E.,**[10] born June 19, 1868, in East Nassau, N. Y.

360 (III) Chloe Ann,[8] daughter of Simon.[7]

Chloe Ann Tifft was married by Rev. A. H. Miller to Marcus Lasher.

Chloe A. Lasher died in Albany, N. Y., Aug. 19, 1857.

CHILDREN OF CHLOE ANN AND MARCUS LASHER.

424 I. **Flavius,**[9]

425 II. **Frank,**[9]

361 (IV) John,[8] son of Simon.[7]

John Tifft, married Jan. 23, 1835, in Nassau, N. Y., by Rev. A. H. Miller, to Sally White, who was born Oct. 18, 1817, in Nassau, N. Y.

John Tifft died Jan. 23, 1852,

Sally Tifft resides in Buffalo, N. Y.

426 I. **Lewis Augustus,**[9] born June 13, 1836, in Nassau, N. Y.

427 II. **James Webster,**[9] born Oct. 15, 1838, in Nassau, N. Y.

428 III. **Pricilla Ann,**[9] born Nov. 2, 1842, in Nassau, N. Y.

429 IV. **Mary Adelia,**[9] born June 23, 1848, in Nassau, N. Y.

---

426 (I) Lewis Augustus,[9] son of John.[8]

Lewis Augustus Tifft, married June 15, 1869, in Springfield, Mass., by Rev. Josiah Marion, to Lurancie Trask, (daughter of ex-Lieutenant-Governor Eliphalet and Ruby Squire Trask) who was born April 16, 1834, in Springfield, Mass.

Lurancie Tifft died Jan. 28, 1869, in Springfield, Mass.

Lewis A. Tifft died Aug. 31, 1874, at Springfield, Mass.

Lewis Augustus Tifft enlisted at Springfield, Sept. 25, 1862, as 2nd Lieut. in Co. A, 46th Regiment M. V. M. Was promoted to 1st Lieut. Nov. 1, 1862, and to the Captaincy Feb. 6, 1863. His service in the 46th Regiment terminated July 29, 1863. He re-enlisted July 13, 1864, as Captain of Co. A, 8th Regiment M. V. M. for 100 days, his services terminating Nov. 10, 1864.

His Company (Co. A, 46th Regiment) assisted in repelling attacks upon Newberne, N. C., and in raising the siege at Little Washington. In an engagement at Batchelders Creek, about seven miles from Newberne, N. C., he, for his judgment and courage, received very favorable mention in the Adjutant-General's report of Massachusetts for 1863.

The Springfield Camp, Sons of Veterans, is named L. A. Tifft Camp in honor of his memory.

He was very prominent in the South Congregational Church, being a member of the building committee which erected the present handsome edifice. He was superintendent and teacher in Hope Chapel Sunday School, one of the South Church branches.

CHILDREN OF LEWIS A. AND LURANCIE TIFFT.

430 I. **Eliphalet Trask,**[10] born June 9, 1860, in Springfield, Mass.

431 II. **Josephine,**[10] born May 8, 1862; died Oct. 11, 1864, in Springfield, Mass.

432 III. **Lurancie,**[10]
433 IV. **Lantie,**[10] } born Jan. 25, 1869, in Springfield, Mass.

---

430 (I) Eliphalet Trask,[10] son of Lewis Augustus.[9]

Eliphalet Trask Tifft, married Oct. 27, 1885, in Springfield, Mass., by Rev. Joseph K. Mason, to Katharine E. Meehan, of Springfield.

Eliphalet T. Tifft attended the public schools of Springfield, graduating from the High School in 1879. After some business experience in the office of a hat factory, he was appointed assistant city clerk and treasurer of Springfield, in August, 1881. In the fall of 1887, he was elected to the position of City Treasurer of Springfiied, which position he has held continuously since, and after the first election he has received the nomination of all parties for the office.

He organized the Collectors' and Treasurers' Association of Massachusetts, of which he fills the position of secretary and treasurer. He is a member of the First Universalist Society, where he has filled various positions. Also a member of L. A. Tifft Camp, Sons of Veterans, and the Springfield Lodge of Masons.

CHILDREN OF ELIPHALET AND KATHARINE E. TIFFT.

434 I. **Lewis Eliphalet,**[11] born Aug. 31, 1886, in Spaingfield, Mass.

435 II. **Charles,**[11] born Sept. 13, 1887, in Springfield, Mass.

432 (III) **Lurancie,**[10] } daughters of
433 (IV) **Lantie,**[10] } Lewis Augustus.[9]

Lurancie and Lantie Tifft were graduated from Springfield High School, and live at Brush Hill, a suburb of Springfield, Mass.

---

427 (II) James Webster,[9] son of John.[8]

James Webster Tifft, married Sept. 22, 1868, in Savannah, N. Y., to Joan C. Palmer, who was born Aug. 15, 1850, in Pineville (Spring Lake), N. Y.

James W. Tifft enlisted as a private in Co. C, 138th N. Y. Volunteers, Infantry, July 2, 1862. He was mustered as 1st Sergeant Sept. 8, 1862. The regiment was changed to 9th N. Y. Volunteer Heavy Artillery, Dec. 9, 1862. He was commissioned 2nd Lieutenant March 10, 1864. At the battle of Monocacy Junction, Md., July 9, 1864, he was severely wounded with gunshot in the left leg; was in the hospital in Baltimore, Md., and at St. Mary's Hospital, Rochester, N. Y., until Nov., 1864, and was honorably discharged Nov. 28, 1864, for wounds received in action.

Residence, Buffalo, N. Y.

CHILDREN OF JAMES WEBSTER AND JOAN C. TIFFT.

436 I. **Loyal W.,**[10] born Aug. 15, 1868, in Spring Lake, N. Y.; died Aug. 28, 1869, in Spring Lake, N. Y.

437 II. **Arthur Palmer,**[10] born Oct. 9, 1872, in Buffalo, N. Y.

---

437 (II) Arthur Palmer,[10] son of James Webster.[9]

Arthur Palmer Tifft is a graduate in pharmacy in the Portland Medical College (Oregon), studied law and was admitted to the bar, June 1896, for the purpose of perfecting himself in the business of associate banking. He was married Nov. 6, 1895,

in Portland, Ore., by Rev. Dr. Henry Basmus, to Maude Akin, who was born Nov. 3, 1876, in Portland, Ore., and attended the St. Helen's Hall School, and is connected with the Portland Flower Mission.

Residence, Mt. Tabor, Portland, Ore.

---

428 (III) Priscilla Ann.[9] daughter of John.[8]

Priscilla Ann Tifft, married Aug. 25, 1885, in Niagara Falls, N. Y., by L. E. Rockwell, to Valda Mere Canfield.

Residence, Buffalo, N. Y.

---

429 (IV) Mary Adelia[9] daughter of John.[8]

Mary Adelia Tifft, married Sept. 19, 1866, in Spring Lake, N. Y., by Rev. N. R. Swift, to Lyman Haley, who was born Sept. 12, 1839, in Spring Lake, N. Y., and died April 10, 1870.

Residence, Buffalo, N. Y.

---

363 (V) Mary,[8] daughter of Simon.[7]

Mary Tifft married April 1, 1843, in Nassau, N. Y., by Rev. R. Collins, to Merriman J. Lester, who was born May 10, 1818, in Chatham, N. Y.

Mary Tifft Lester died in Hoag's Corners, N.Y., March 19, 1888.

Merriman Lester died in Hoag's Corners, N. Y., Jan. 12, 1894.

CHILDREN OF MARY AND MERRIMAN LESTER.

438 I. **Webster T.,**[9] born April 21, 1844, in Hoag's Corners; died April 11, 1845, in Hoag's Corners.

439 II. **Sophia,**[9] born April 2, 1847, in Hoag's Corners.

440 III. **George W. T.,**[9] born Oct. 31, 1849, in Hoag's Corners.

441 IV. **Charles G.,**[9] born Nov. 11, 1854, in Nassau, N. Y.

442 V. **Fred. J.,**[9] born Sept. 20, 1857, in Buffalo, N. Y.

439 (II) Sophia,[9] daughter of Mary.[8]

Sophia Lester, married April 15, 1879, in Hoag's Corners by Rev. I B. Coleman, to Albert H. Crawford, M. D., who was graduated from the University of Buffalo and has held the office of Coronor.

Residence, Buffalo, N. Y.

CHILDREN OF SOPHIA AND ALBERT H. CRAWFORD.

443 I. **Florence Albertine,**[10] born March 28, 1883, in Buffalo, N. Y.

444 II. **Marion Eloise,**[10] born May 11, 1884, in Buffalo, N. Y.

---

440 (III) George W. T.,[9] son of Mary.[8]

George W. T. Lester, married Oct. 5, 1876, in Hoag's Corners, by Rev. I. B. Coleman, to Ella V. Coleman, who was born June 3, 1852, in Boonville, N. Y.

Residence, Hoag's Corners, N. Y.

CHILDREN OF GEO. W. T. AND ELLA LESTER.

445 I. **Howard Coleman,**[10] born Nov. 19, 1877, in Hoag's Corners.

446 II. **Elvira Mary,**[10] born April 29, 1883, in Dunham Hollow.

447 III. **Guy Merriman,**[10] born May 30, 1890, in Hoag's Corners.

---

441 (IV) Charles G.,[9] son of Mary.[8]

Charles G. Lester, married June 25, 1879, in —— —— by Rev. J. Zweifel, to Elizabeth A. Williams, who was born July 22, 1859, in Nassau, N. Y.

Residence, Hoag's Corners, N.Y.

---

442 (V) Fred J.,[9] son of Mary.[8]

Fred J. Lester, married March 25, 1883, in Sand Lake, N. Y., by Rev. J. Martin, to Emma Finkell, who was born in 1864, in Sand Lake, N. Y.

Emma Lester died March 14, 1891, in Buffalo, N. Y.

Fred J. Lester married a second time Dec. 29, 1892, by Rev. Mr. Fallon, to Mrs. Rose Farron.

Residence, Buffalo, N. Y.

CHILDREN OF FRED J. AND EMMA LESTER.

448 I. **Alice Minerva,**[10] born March 14, 1884, in Hoag's Corners.

449 II. **Florence,**[10] born Aug, 30, 1886, in Hoag's Corners; died Dec. 26, 1892, in Buffalo, N. Y.

360 (VI) Abbie,[8] daughter of Simon.[7]

Abbie Tifft, married Jan. 14, 1840, in Nassau, N. Y., by Rev. I. B. Coleman, to Dennis Lewis, who was born Aug. 26, 1818, and died May 22, 1874, in Nassau, N. Y.

Dennis Lewis was Justice of the Peace at East Nassau twenty years; postmaster at same place twenty-four years; Superintendent of the Poor one term, and Supervisor one term; Trustee of Presbyterian Church at East Nassau from the time the church was built until the time of his death.

Residence, East Nassau, N. Y.

CHILDREN OF ABBEY G. W. AND DENNIS LEWIS.

450 I. **Hazard,**[9] born Nov. 1, 1840, in Nassau, N. Y.; died March 30, 1841, in Nassau, N. Y.

451 II. **Bertha Sophelia,**[9] born July 31, 1844, in Nassau, N.Y.

452 III. **Mary Eliza,**[9] born Dec. 18, 1847, in Nassau, N. Y.

453 IV. **John,**[9] born Feb. 27, 1853, in Nassau, N. Y.; died March 27, 1856, in Nassau, N. Y.

451 (II) Bertha Sophelia,[9] daughter of Abbie.[8]

Bertha Sophelia Lewis, married March 7, 1866, in Nassau, N.Y., by Rev. I. N. Collins, to John Knox Harder, who was born March 6, 1840, in Nassau, N. Y.

Residence, Malden Bridge, N. Y.

CHILDREN OF BERTHA SOPHELIA AND JOHN K. HARDER.

454 I. **Mary Lewis,**[10] born May 30, 1868, in E. Nassau, N. Y.; died April 7, 1875, in Nassau, N. Y.

455 II. **Edna K.,**[10] born Oct. 14, 1875, in Malden Bridge, N. Y.

---

455 (II) Edna K.,[10] daughter of Bertha Sophelia.[9]

Edna K. Harder was graduated from Chatham Academy June 19, 1894.

---

452 (III) Mary Eliza,[9] daughter of Abbie.[8]

Mary Eliza Lewis, married Dec. 18, 1865, in East Nassau, N.Y., by Rev. I. N. Collier, to Jared Lester Root Davis, who was born April 21, 1844, in West Lebanon, N. Y.

Mary Eliza Davis died in East Nassau, March 8, 1891.

Jared Lester Root Davis resides in East Nassau, N. Y.

---

365 (VIII) Wrilson Simon,[8] son of Simon.[7]

Wrilson Simon Tifft, married Feb. 12, 1856, in Lyons, N.Y., by Rev. T. B. Hudson, to Cynthia S. Lester, who was born Sept. 15, 1835, in Palmyra, N. Y., and died in Buffalo, N.Y., Feb. 5, 1873.

Wrilson S. Tifft married a second time July 5, 1874, in Adams, N. Y., by Rev. H. W. Bennett, to Maria Elizabeth Maxon, who was born June 5, 1856, in Adams, N. Y.

Wrilson S. Tifft's early days were spent on his father's farm, and at work in his father's sawmill. He attended the district school, in the days when the teachers boarded round with the families in the district, and the boys built the fires in the schoolhouse in winter.

In the spring of 1849, at the age of twenty-four, Mr. Tifft came to Buffalo, to visit his uncle Geo. W. Tifft, which resulted in his becoming a citizen of this city. He engaged in the retail milk business, which was soon changed to a wholesale trade and he supplied grocers, hotels, and the large passenger propellers, which ran in the lakes at that time. In 1872 he retired from any active engagement in the milk business and since then, has devoted his time to his real estate interests.

Mr. Tifft is one of the many self-made men in Buffalo, who, by indomitable perseverance and business energy, have attained success. Helpful to those less fortunate than himself, where he saw the need; giving generously where least expected. He was a member of and served Grace M. E. Church as trustee for about fifteen years.

Maria E. Tifft has been a member of the Women's Educational and Industrial Union of Buffalo since its organization; is one of its active members, being on the Library Committee, and is a life member of that Society. She is also engaged in the work of the Buffalo Deaconess' Home of the Genesee Conference of the Methodist Episcopal Church, being a member of the Conduct of Home Committee of that organization.

Residence, 196 Linwood Ave., Buffalo, N. Y.

CHILDREN OF WRILSON S. AND CYNTHIA S. TIFFT.

456 I. **Jennie,**[9] born May 23, 1859, in Buffalo, N. Y.; died Nov. 4, 1861, in Buffalo, N. Y.

457 II. **Charles Lester,**[9] born Oct. 26, 1862, in Buffalo, N. Y.; died Oct. 2, 1870, in Buffalo, N. Y.

458 III. **Curtis Gay,**[9] born April 9, 1866, in Buffalo, N. Y.; died Nov. 3, 1870, in Buffalo, N. Y.

CHILDREN OF WRILSON S., AND MARIA E. TIFFT.

459 IV. **Maxon Wrilson,**[9] born March 24, 1875, in Buffalo, N. Y.

460 V. **Lilian Vary,**[9] born June 28, 1877, in Buffalo, N. Y.; died May 16, 1888.

461 VI. **Robert Hull,**[9] born June 23, 1886.

---

459 (IV) Maxon Wrilson,[9] son of Wrilson Simon.[8]

Maxon Wrilson Tifft entered the Law Department of the University of Buffalo, Class of 1897.

---

366 (IX) Frances Sophia,[8] daughter of Simon.[7]

Frances Sophia Tifft, married ——— Nassau, N. Y., to Francis Burdick, who died June 15, 1870.

Frances Sophia Burdick died Sept. 3, 1855, in East Nassau, N.Y.

CHILDREN OF FRANCES SOPHIA AND FRANCIS BURDICK.

462 I. **Freeland,**[9] born Aug. 15, 1853.

463 II. **Lewis,**[9] born Aug. 9, 1855.

---

460 (III) Lewis,[9] son of Frances Sophia.[8]

Lewis Burdick, married Nov. 6, 1878, in Harlan, Iowa, by Rev. G. Parker, to Lizzie M. Stokes, who was born Jan. 11, 1862, in Rock Island, Ill.

Residence, Kearney, Neb.

CHILDREN OF LEWIS AND LIZZIE BURDICK.

464 I. **Lewis W.,**[10] born March 18, 1880, in Harlan, Iowa.

465 II. **Grace L.,**[10] born Nov. 21, 1882, in Harlan, Iowa.

195 (V) Polly,[7] daughter of John.[6]

Polly Tifft lived with her brother, Sprague Tifft, in Nassau, N.Y., and died there June 23, 1835, unmarried.

196 (VI) David,[7] son of John.[6]

David Tifft, married June 8, 1809, in Nassau, N. Y., to Charlotte Smith, who was born Jan. 19, 1793, and died Feb. 26, 1849, in Nassau, N. Y.

David Tifft married a second time, Aug. 6, 1851, in Veteran, N. Y., by Rev. S. C. Wetherby, to Emily Elwell.

During the War of 1812 David Tifft enlisted, and on the Captain's return home, served in his place. The Regiment started for Plattsburg, but were recalled and discharged before reaching that place.

He died Oct. 17, 1854, in Veteran, N. Y.

CHILDREN OF DAVID AND CHARLOTTE TIFFT.

466 I. **Reuben Smith,**[8] born July 7, 1810, in Nassau, N. Y.

467 II. **Joanna Smith,**[8] born Oct. 23, 1812, in Nassau, N. Y.

468 III. **Harriet Maria,**[8] born July 31, 1814, in Nassau, N. Y.

469 IV. **William S.,**[8] born April 28, 1816, in Nassau, N. Y.

470 V. **Miranda Lewis,**[8] born April 2, 1818, in Nassau, N. Y.

471 VI. **Edwin Vallett,**[8] born Feb. 9, 1820, in Nassau, N. Y.

472 VII. **Delia Barnum,**[8] born Feb. 28, 1822, in Nassau, N. Y.

473 VIII. **David Russell,**[8] born May 1, 1824, in Nassau, N. Y.

474 IX. **Charlotte M.,**[8] born July 13, 1826; died Nov. 15, 1826, in Nassau, N. Y.

CHILD OF DAVID AND EMILY TIFFT.

475 X. **George Alanson,**[8] born July 6, 1852, in Veteran, N.Y. died Jan. 3, 1863, in Veteran, N. Y.

466 (I) Reuben Smith,[8] son of David.[7]

Reuben Smith Tifft, married Jan. 7, 1830, in Nassau, N. Y., to Sally Turner, who was born in Nassau March 2, 1811, and died in Veteran, N. Y., Oct. 26, 1864.

Reuben Smith Tifft married a second time May 6, 1867, in Veteran, N. Y., by Rev. S. C. Wetherby, to Lucinda Martha Coleman, who was born in Veteran June 27, 1838.

Reuben S. Tifft with four others moved from Rensselaer County to Chemung County in Feb., 1829, with wagons drawn by oxen, being on the way thirteen days. They encountered snow drifts, rain, hailstorms and mud. Their last stopping place was Newtown (Elmira), where the mud so encased the wheels of their wagons that on the following morning there were no spaces between the spokes—it had frozen solid during the night. When they reached their new home they found but one framed house in the vicinity. The schoolhouse, as well as dwelling houses, were made of logs. They attended worship on Sunday in a barn, and experienced such other privations as pioneers usually meet. Reuben S. Tiflt served as Supervisor of the town of Veteran, was Highway Commissioner, and a member of the Board of Judges at the Chemung County Agricultural Fair for live stock, for a number of years.

He died in Veteran, N. Y., Nov. 13, 1888.

CHILDREN OF REUBEN SMITH AND SALLY TIFFT.

476 I. **Charlotte Katharine,**[9] born Feb. 16, 1831, in Veteran, N. Y.

477 II. **John Benjamin,**[9] born Nov. 10, 1832, in Veteran, N. Y.

478 III. **David Edwin,**[9] born Nov. 10, 1832.

479 IV. **Reuben,**[9] born Feb. 19, 1835.

480 V. **William Miller,**[9] born Sept. 19, 1837; died Feb. 27, 1851.

481 VI. **Sally M.,**[9] born May 27, 1840, in Veteran, N. Y.; died Jan. 4, 1841.

482 VII. **Chloe Angeline,**[9] born March 13, 1843, in Veteran, N. Y.

483 VIII. **Lucretia Sarah,**[9] born Jan. 6, 1846, in Veteran, N.Y.

484 IX. **Harvey M.,**[9] born July 29, 1854, in Veteran, N. Y.

CHILDREN OF REUBEN SMITH AND LUCINDA TIFFT.

485 X. **Grant Lincoln,**[9] born Dec. 6, 1868.

486 XI. **Ulysses Dent,**[9] born July 15, 1871, in Veteran, N.Y.; died July 8, 1872.

487 XII. **Wilson D.,**[9] born Aug. 23, 1873, in Veteran, N. Y.; died May 20, 1884.

488 XIII. **Anna Lena,**[9] born May 1, 1880.

---

476 (I) Charlotte Katharine,[9] daughter of Reuben Smith.[8]

Charlotte Katharine Tifft, married Jan. 13, 1853, in Veteran, N. Y., by Rev. S. C. Wetherby, to Norman Wood, who was born in Veteran, Dec. 2, 1827.

Residence, Veteran, N. Y.

CHILD OF CHARLOTTE K. AND NORMAN WOOD.

489 I. **Willis Tifft,**[10] born July 20, 1863, in Veteran, N. Y.

---

474 (II) John Benjamin,[9] son of Reuben Smith.[8]

John Benjamin Tifft, married Jan. 17, 1861, by Rev. Mr. Coffin, in Big Flats, N. Y., to Betsey Briggs, who was born in Big Flats, N. Y., Aug. 7, 1835.

John B. Tifft enlisted in the army during the Civil War, in the spring of 1865; went into camp at Elmira, N. Y., but was soon mustered out.

Residence, Big Flats, N. Y.

---

478 (III) David Edwin,[9] son of Reuben Smith.[8]

David Edwin Tifft, married Oct. 7, 1860, in Veteran, N. Y., by Rev. S. C. Wetherby, to Margaret A. Dufur, who was born in Catlin, N. Y.

Residence, Elmira, N. Y.

CHILDREN OF DAVID E. AND MARGARET TIFFT.

490 I. **Fred. Miller,**[10] born Aug. 19, 1861, in Veteran, N. Y.; died June 2, 1862.

491 II. **George B.,**[10] born Feb. 6, 1863.

492 III. **Sarah Ellen,**[10] born Feb. 22, 1865, in Veteran, N. Y.

493 IV. **Laura Amelia,**[10] born Aug. 1, 1868, in Veteran, N.Y.

494 V. **Lottie W.,**[10] born March 2, 1871, in Veteran, N. Y.; died Jan. 10, 1888, in Elmira, N. Y.

495 VI. **Mary E.,**[10] born May 1, 1874, in Veteran, N. Y.

496 VII. **Ettie May,**[10] born Aug. 17, 1875, in Catlin, N. Y.

497 VIII. **Adella E.,**[10] born May 19, 1877, in Catlin, N. Y.

498 IX. **Lucinda A.,**[10] born Aug. 6, 1878, in Erin, N. Y.

499 X. **Ruby L.,**[10] born Jan. 19, 1880, in Horseheads, N. Y.

500 XI. **Edna P.,**[10] born May 1, 1882, in Horseheads, N. Y.; died Aug. 4, 1882.

---

491 (II) George B.,[10] son of David Edwin.[9]

George B. Tifft, married July 4, 1885, in Binghamton, N.Y., by John W. Frost, J P., to Anna Foraker.

---

492 (III) Sarah Ellen,[10] daughter of David Edwin.[9]

Sarah Ellen Tifft, married March 18, 1880, in Veteran, N. Y., by R. C. Wetherby, to Lewis McIntyre.

---

493 (IV) Laura Amelia,[10] daughter of David Edwin.[9]

Laura Amelia Tifft, married Nov. 27, 1889, in Elmira, N. Y., by Rev. W. T. Henry, D. D., to Henry J. Baltz.

---

495 (VI) Mary E.,[10] daughter of David Edwin.[9]

Mary E. Tifft, married Oct. 17, 1892, in Elmira, N. Y., by Rev. W. T. Henry, D. D., to Herbert Baty.

---

479 (IV) Reuben,[9] son of Reuben Smith.[8]

Reuben Tifft, married Sept. 15, 1856, in Southport, N. Y., by Rev. Mr. Huntley, to Emaline Rebecca Crane, who was born in Bennetsburg, N. Y., Nov. 24, 1832. Residence, Horseheads, N. Y.

CHILDREN OF REUBEN AND EMALINE R. TIFFT.

501 I. **Mary Anna,**[10] } born Nov. 23, 1858, in Pine Valley,
502 II. **Bela Crane,**[10] } N. Y.

---

501 (I) Mary Anna,[10] daughher of Reuben.[9]

Mary Anna Tifft, married Dec. 28, 1881, in Horseheads, N. Y., by Rev. T. S. Phillips, to Harvey J. Coleman, who was born in Troy, N. Y. Residence, Horseheads, N. Y.

CHILDREN OF MARY ANNA AND HARVEY J. COLEMAN.

503 I. **Reuben G.,**[11] born June 1, 1885, in Horseheads, N. Y.; died March 19, 1888.

504 II. **Archie Donald,**[11] born July 5, 1887, in Breesport, N.Y.; died Aug. 1, 1890.

505 III. **Urania, Marion,**[11] born Nov. 21, 1890.

---

502 (II) Bela Crane,[10] son of Reuben.[9]

Bela Crane Tifft, married Dec. 18, 1890, in Breesport, by Rev. H. B. Clark, to Winifred Jansen, who was born Nov. 3, 1871, in Breesport. Residence, Horseheads, N. Y.

CHILD OF BELA C. AND WINIFRED TIFFT.

506 I. **Harry Jansen,**[11] born in Horseheads, N.Y., Sept. 23, 1891.

---

482 (VII), Chloe Angeline,[9] daughter of Reuben Smith.[8]

Chloe Angeline Tifft, married Feb. 14, 1866, in Horseheads, N. Y., by Rev. P. Olney, to John Bale Rays, who was born in Sparta, Sussex County, N. J., May 4, 1838, and who served his country as a Union soldier in the Civil War of 1861-5.

Residence, Veteran, N. Y.

---

483 (VIII) Lucretia Sarah,[9] daughter of Reuben Smith.[8]

Lucretia Sarah Tifft, married Feb. 14, 1866, in Horseheads, N. Y., by Rev. P. Olney, to Ezra Howell, who was born in Tyrone, N. Y., in 1840.

Residence, Horseheads, N. Y.

CHILD OF LUCRETIA S. AND EZRA HOWELL.

507 I. **Iona May,**[10] born Feb. 23, 1873, in Veteran, N. Y.

---

484 (IX) Harvey M.,[9] son of Reuben Smith.[8]

Harvey M. Tifft, married Nov. 19, 1876, in Veteran, N. Y., by Rev. S. C. Wetherby, to Emma E. Anthony, who was born in Elmira, N. Y., Dec. 28, 1853.

Residence, Horseheads, N. Y.

CHILDREN OF HARVEY M. AND EMMA E. TIFFT.

508 I. **Elmer Anthony,**[10] born Feb. 3, 1879, in Veteran, N.Y.

509 II. **Lester H.,**[10] } born May 2, 1883, in Veteran, N. Y.;

510 III. **Luther M.,**[10] } died May 29, 1883.

467 (II) Joanna Smith,[8] daughter of David.[7]

Joanna Smith Tifft, married Feb. 24, 1831, in Nassau, N.Y., by Rev. A. H. Miller, to Samuel Coleman Wetherby, who was born in West Stephentown, N. Y., March 27, 1810.

Samuel C. Wetherby gave evidence while a boy that he possessed the preacher's instinct, and it is said that he and Isaiah Coleman, when boys, held meetings, carrying out the usual exercises with the regularity manifested by older Christians. He served the Stephentown and Nassau Church of the Free Will Baptist denomination for twelve years as a deacon, and was ordained a minister of the gospel by that church April 16, 1843. He served three churches ten years each, Veteran, Dix and Pine Valley, aiding largely in the erection of the church at the last-named place, and by his untiring zeal was the means, to a great degree, of helping the church there to an independent standing in the denomination.

He cheerfully contributed of his means to the furtherance of the gospel, and always manifested a self-sacrificing spirit for the cause he loved. During his ministry he officiated in the Tifft families at the marriages of parents, children and grandchildren. He wrought for his Master in the ministry thirty-three years, and went to his grave ripe for the harvest, July 25, 1877, in Veteran, N. Y.

Joanna S. Wetherby died July 20, 1895, in Big Flats, N. Y.

CHILD OF JOANNA S. AND SAMUEL C. WETHERBY.

511 I. **Harriet Maria,**[9] born Dec. 16, 1836, in Nassau, N. Y.

511 (I) Harriet Maria,[9] daughter of Joanna Smith.[8]

Harriet Maria Wetherby, married May 18, 1891, in Pine Valley, N. Y., by Rev. H. Ream, to Orlando Groom, who was born May 4, 1825, in Veteran, N. Y.

Residence, Big Flats, N. Y.

---

468 (III) Harriet Maria,[8] daughter of David.[8]

Harriet Maria Tifft, married Sept. 10, 1836, in Nassau, N.Y., by Rev. S. C. Wetherby, to Martin Wheeler, who was born in West Stephentown, N. Y., July 16, 1814.

Harriet Maria Wheeler died in Veteran, Oct. 6, 1882.

Martin Wheeler died in Odessa, N. Y., Aug. 27, 1890.

CHILD OF HARRIET M. AND MARTIN WHEELER.

512 I. **Charlotte Ann,**[9] born Nov. 5, 1837, in Nassau, N. Y.

---

512 (I) Charlotte Ann,[9] daughter of Harriet Maria.[8]

Carlotte Ann Wheeler, married April 18, 1855, in Veteran, N.Y. by Rev. S. C. Wetherby, to Benjamin Turner, who was born April 1, 1834, in Veteran, N. Y.

Residence, Veteran, N. Y.

CHILDREN OF CHARLOTTE ANN AND BENJAMIN TURNER.

513 I. **Hattie Electa,**[10] born April 14, 1855, in Veteran, N.Y.

514 II. **Harvey Martin,**[10] born June 4, 1858, in Veteran, N.Y.; died July 23, 1858.

515 III. **Edward Martin,**[10] born May 1, 1860, in Veteran, N.Y.

516 IV. **Fred Benjamin,**[10] born June 20, 1865, in Veteran, N.Y.

517 V. **Louisa May,**[10] born June 13, 1868, in Veteran, N. Y.

518 VI. **Dexter,**[10] born Nov. 1, 1875, in Veteran, N. Y.; died Feb. 16, 1876.

519 VII. **George Archie,**[10] born Jan. 16, 1877, in Veteran, N.Y.

513 (I) Hattie Electa,[10] daughter of Charlotte Ann.

Hattie Electa Turner, married Nov. 25, 1874, in Veteran, N.Y., by Rev. S. C. Wetherby, to Edwin Miller, who was born in Newark Valley, N. Y., June 30, 1856.

Residence, Veteran, N. Y.

CHILDREN OF HATTIE E. AND EDWIN MILLER.

520 I. **Edna,** [11] born March 7, 1879, in Veteran, N. Y., died Feb. 18, 1893.

---

515 (III) Edward Martin,[10] son of Charlotte Ann.[9]

Edward Martin Turner, married Dec. 25, 1878, in Veteran, N. Y., by Rev. E. B. Collins, to Celia E. Miller, who was born in Millport, N. Y., March 8, 1860. Residence, Veteran, N. Y.

CHILDREN OF EDWARD M. AND CELIA E. TURNER.

521 I. **Edith L.,**[11] born Oct. 15, 1879, in Veteran, N. Y.

522 II. **Benjamin F.,**[11] born Aug. 12, 1889, in Veteran, N. Y.

---

516 (IV) Fred Benjamin,[10] son of Charlotte Ann.[9]

Fred Benjamin Turner, married Nov. 5, 1888, in Veteran, N.Y., by Rev. E. B. Collins, to Anna Cooley, who was born in Millport, N. Y., April 23, 1865. Residence, Elmira, N. Y.

CHILD OF FRED B. AND ANNA TURNER.

523 I. **Myrta Charlotte,**[11] born Nov. 27, 1889, in Veteran, N. Y.

---

517 (V) Louisa May,[10] daughter of Charlotte Ann.[9]

Louisa May Turner, married Dec. 25, 1885, in Veteran, N. Y., by Rev. C. L. Cornell, to Frank Doolittle, who was born in Odessa, N. Y., Dec. 28, 1862.

Residence, Veteran, N. Y.

CHILDREN OF LOUISA MAY AND FRANK DOOLITTLE.

524 I. **Lottie,**[11] born March 27, 1886, in Veteran, N. Y.

525 II. **Helen,**[11] born Nov. 1, 1889, in Veteran, N. Y.

469 (IV) William S.,[8] son of David.[7]

William S. Tifft, married April 28, 1839, in Stephentown, N.Y., by Rev. I. B. Coleman, to Cordelia H. Brainard, who was born in Stephentown April 30, 1829, and died in Millport April 28, 1878.

William S. Tifft, married a second time Jan. 22, 1880, in Millport, N. Y.; by Rev. J. R. Hutchins, to Phebe Ann Carr, who was born in Tireton, Ohio, Oct. 12, 1843.

William S. Tifft served his town as Highway Commissioner twelve years and has been one of the Trustees of the Baptist Church at Millport over twenty years.

Residence, Millport, N. Y.

CHILDREN OF WILLIAM S. AND CORDELIA H. TIFFT.

526 I. **William Alonzo,**[9] born March 23, 1840, in Stephentown, N. Y.

527 II. **Nathan Henry,**[9] born April 1, 1844, in Stephentown, N.Y.

528 III. **David Brainard,**[9] born Dec. 5, 1847, in Stephentown, N. Y.

526 (I) William Alonzo,[9] son of William S.[8]

William Alonzo Tifft, married March 23, 1868, in West Sand Lake, N. Y., by Rev. M. W. Empie to Agnes M. Green, who was born in North Greenbush, Dec. 26, 1844.

William Alonzo Tifft was a graduate of Lowell's Business College, Binghampton, N. Y. Trustee of the Millport Baptist Church a number of years.

William Alonzo Tifft died in Millport, N. Y., May 20, 1886.

527 (II) Nathan Henry,[9] son of William S.[8]

Nathan Henry Tifft enlisted during the Civil War in 1862 in the 125th Regiment, N. Y. S. V., Col. Willard commanding officer. He was in two engagements, the surrender of Harper's Ferry and Weldon R. R., Va.; in hospital two months, after which he was honorably discharged.

---

528 (III) David Brainard,[9] son of William S.[8]

David Brainard Tifft, married Dec. 25, 1873, in Millport, N.Y., by Rev. J. T. Canfield, to Louisa Strunk, who was born in Minden Waser Valley, Germany.

CHILD OF DAVID B. AND LOUISA TIFFT.

529 I. **Lottie Cordelia,**[10] born Jan. 8, 1874, in Millport, N. Y.

---

470 (V) Miranda Lewis,[8] daughter of David.[7]

Miranda Lewis Tifft, married Sept. 23, 1840, in Nassau, N.Y., by Rev. I. B. Coleman to James Harvey Coleman, who was born in Stephentown, N. Y., July 22, 1816.

Miranda L. Coleman, died in Veteran, N. Y., April 28, 1889.

James H. Coleman, died in Veteran, N. Y., July 17, 1895.

---

471 (V) Edwin Vallett,[8] son of David.[7]

Edwin Vallett Tifft, married July 8, 1843 in Nassau, N. Y., by Rev. S. C. Wetherby, to Priscilla Ann Barber, who was born in Nassau, Nov. 23. 1820, and died in Veteran, N. Y., March 7, 1852.

Edwin Vallett Tifft, married a second time Sept 28, 1863, in Hornellsville, N. Y., by Rev. S. G. Bowles, to Marion Serena Lamb, who was born in Lebanon, N. Y., Aug. 4, 1835.

Edwin V. Tifft has been a deacon in the Baptist Church of Millport, N. Y., for 18 years, and has served that church as Trustee for twelve years.

Marion S. L. Tifft has been identified with the educational and temperance work in Chemung County, N. Y., for a period of thirty years. Her education was finished at the Young Ladies' Seminary of Oneida, N. Y. While teaching she frequently read papers on some phase of ethics as related to the schools before Teachers' Institutes, and also addressed teachers on the subject of temperance teaching. Served as Secretary for the Teachers' Association, and was a member of the committee for uniformity of text books in Chemung County, N. Y. She served in the Women's Christian Temperance Union as local and county officer and as State Superintendent of Scientific Temperance Institution. Also served as leader in the Foreign Mission work of the Baptist Church.

CHILDREN OF EDWIN V. AND PRISCILLA TIFFT.

530 I. **Charles Edwin,**[9] born June 26, 1844, in Nassau, N. Y.

531 II. **Emily Frances,**[9] born Jan. 15, 1846, in Hancock, Mass.

532 III. **Cyrus R.,**[9] born July 20, 1848, in Nassau, N. Y.; died July 12, 1865, in Veteran, N. Y.

533 IV. **Mary Adelia,**[9] born July 11, 1850, in Veteran, N. Y.

---

520 (I) Charles Edwin,[9] son of Edwin Vallett.[8]

Charles Edwin Tifft, married March 6, 1867 in Veteran, N. Y., by Rev. S. C. Wetherby, to Olive Adelia Vangorden, who was born in Starkey, N, Y., Jan. 27, 1845.

Residence, New York City.

CHILDREN OF CHARLES EDWIN AND OLIVE A. TIFFT.

534 I. **Cyrus Albert,**[10] born Oct. 28, 1868, in Veteran, N. Y.

535 II. **Grace Adella,**[10] born May 17, 1870, in Veteran, N. Y.

536 III. **Eva Laura,**[10] born Feb 7, 1873, in Fleming, N. Y.
537 IV. **James Edwin,**[10] born June 30, 1877, in Fleming, N. Y.

---

534 (I) Cyrus Albert,[10] son of Charles Edwin.[9]

Cyrus Albert Tifft, married Feb. 14, 1891, in Brooklyn, N. Y., by Rev. Mr. McGuire, to Lucy Maria Jordan, who was born in Brooklyn, N. Y., June 28, 1871.

---

535 (II Grace Adella,[10] daughter of Charles Edwin.[9]

Grace Adella Tifft, married Nov. 17, 1892, in Fleming, N. Y., by Rev. Mr. Barnes to Linn C. Herrick.
Residence, Fleming, N. Y.

CHILD OF GRACE A. AND LINN C. HERRICK.

538 I. **Olive Alida,**[11] born Dec. 1, 1893, in Park Settlement, N.Y.

---

536 (III) Eva Laura,[10] daughter of Charles Edwin.[9]

Eva Laura Tifft, married March 18, 1895, in New York City, by Rev. T. Skinner, to William Cook, who was born Jan. 20, 1875, in Elizabethport, N. J.

Residence, New York City.

537 (IV) James Edwin,[10] son of Charles Edwin.[9]

---

531 (II) Emily Frances,[9] daughter of Edwin Vallett.[8]

Emily Frances Tifft, married April 16, 1866 in Veteran, N. Y., by Rev. D. M. Rollins to Leonard Elmer Dufur, who was born in Cantlin, N. Y., June 6, 1848.

Leonard E. Dufur served his country as a Union soldier in the Civil War. He died in Brooklyn, N. Y., July 22, 1879.

CHILDREN OF EMILY F. AND LEONARD E. DUFUR.

539 I. **Anna Bell,**[10] born April 11. 1867, in Veteran, N. Y.

540 II. **Mary Ella,**[10] born Nov. 6, 1869, in Veteran, N. Y.

---

539 (I) Anna Bell,[10] daughter of Emily Frances.[9]

Anna Bell Dufur, married Oct. 2, 1885, in Brooklyn, N. Y., by Rev. Mr. McKellogg, to Edward Jerome Gray.

CHILDREN OF ANNA B. AND EDWARD J. GRAY.

541 I. **Emma Amelia,**[11] born July 27, 1886, in Brooklyn, N. Y.; died July 16, 1887, in Brooklyn, N. Y.

542 II. **Nettie Viola,**[11] born July 28, 1888, in Brooklyn, N. Y.

543 III. **Victor,**[11] born June 30, 1890, in Brooklyn, N. Y.

---

540 (II) Mary Ella,[10] daughter of Emily Frances.[9]

Mary Ella Dufur, married in Brooklyn, N. Y., May 7, 1888, by Rev. Mr. McKellogg, to Edward Patrick Walsh.

Residence, Brooklyn, N. Y.

CHILDREN OF MARY E. AND EDWARD P. WALSH.

544 I. **Charles Wm. Dufur,**[11] born May 13, ——, in Brooklyn, N. Y.

545 II. **Edwin V. Dufur,**[11] born April 14, ——, in Brooklyn, N. Y.

546 III. **Edith May,**[11] born Aug. 24, ——, in Brooklyn, N. Y.

547 IV. **Bertha Adella,**[11] born Dec. 25, ——, in Brooklyn, N.Y.

---

533 (IV) Mary Adelia,[9] daughter of Edwin Vallett.[8]

Mary Adelia Tifft, married March 27, 1872, in Veteran, N. Y., by Rev. S. C. Wetherby to William Holtz, who was born in Mecklenburg, Germany, Oct. 3, 1844.

Residence, Elmira, N. Y.

CHILDREN OF MARY A. AND WILLIAM HOLTZ.

548 I. **Etta May,**[10] born Jan. 4, 1874, in Horseheads, N. Y.

549 II. **Ella,**[10] born July 29, 1877, in Veteran, N. Y.

550 III. **Luther,**[10] born Oct. 1, 1882, in Veteran, N. Y.

551 IV. **Lena Eva,**[10] born Aug. 8, 1886, in Kalamazoo, Mich.

---

472 (VII) Delia Barnum,[8] daughter of David.[7]

Delia Barnum Tifft, married May 4, 1838, in Nassau, N. Y., by Rev. A. H. Miller, to Reuben Wait.

Delia Barnum Wait died Nov. 18, 1847, in Sand Lake, N. Y.

CHILDREN OF DELIA AND REUBEN WAIT.

552 I. **Martha Ann,**[9] born June 1, 1839, in Nassau, N. Y.; died (date not known.)

553 II. **Melissa,**[9] born June 3, 1845, in Nassau, N. Y.

---

553 (II) Melissa,[9] daughter of Delia Barnum.[8]

Melissa Wait, married Oct. 24, 1863, in Veteran, N.Y., by Rev. S. C. Wetherby, to Luther Green.

Melissa Wait Green died July 2, 1871, in Veteran, N. Y.

CHILD OF MELISSA AND LUTHER GREEN.

554 I. **William,**[10] born in Alba, Pa., July 3, 1866.

---

473 (VIII) David Russell,[8] son of David.[7]

David Russell Tifft, married May 13, 1852, in Veteran, N.Y., by Rev. S. C. Wetherby, to Mary A. Durbon, who was born in Ulysses, N. Y., Feb. 3, 1829.

CHILDREN OF DAVID R. AND MARY A. TIFFT.

555 I. **William Fred,**[9] Jan. 17, 1855, in Veteran, N. Y.

556 II. **Delia Lilian,**[9] born March 5, 1857, in Veteran, N. Y.

557 III. **Frank Richard,**[9] born Sept. 2, 1859, in Veteran, N. Y.
558 IV. **Katie Emeliza,**[9] born Oct. 4, 1862, in Veteran, N. Y.
559 V. **Rose Lottie,**[9] born Sept. 5, 1866, in Veteran, N. Y.

---

555 (I) William Fred,[9] son of David Russell.[8]

William Fred Tifft, married Jan. 5, 1891 in Horseheads, N. Y., by Rev. C. C. Carr to Hattie May Burton, who was born in Cameron, N. Y., Feb. 11, 1872.

CHILDREN OF WILLIAM FRED AND HATTIE M. TIFFT.

560 I. **Mary Augusta,**[10] born Feb. 13, 1892, in Big Flats, N, Y.
561 II. **Anna Rose,**[10] born Sept. 5, 1893, in Big Flats, N. Y.
562 III. **Teresa Amelia,**[10] born Nov. 14, 1895, in Big Flats, N. Y.

---

556 (II) Delia Lilian,[9] daughter of David Russell.[8]

Delia Lilian Tifft is a graduate of Cook Academy, Havana, N. Y., married May 13, 1884, in Big Flats, N. Y., by Rev. H. S. Jewell to John C. Hadley, who was born in Jackson, Pa., April 18, 1862.

Residence, Rochester, N. Y.

CHILD OF DELIA L. AND JOHN C. HADLEY.

563 I. **Hattie May,**[10] born March 16, 1895, in Rochester, N. Y.

---

557 (III) Frank Richard,[9] son of David Russell.[8]

Frank Richard Tifft, married Jan 24, 1890, in Horseheads, N. Y., by Rev. C. C. Carr, to Hattie Lorena Davis, who was born in Wisconsin April 3, 1868.

---

558 (IV) Katie Emeliza,[9] daughter of David Russell.[8]

Katie Emeliza Tifft, married Oct. 26, 1881, in Big Flats, N. Y., by Rev. H. S. Jewell, to Nathan H. Fosdick, who was born in Howells, N. Y., May 15, 1858.

Residence, Big Flats, N. Y.

CHILDREN OF KATIE E. AND NATHAN H. FOSDICK.

564 I. **Raymond Tifft,**[10] born Jan. 2, 1883, in Big Flats, N. Y.
565 II. **Lewis Henry,**[10] born Jan. 12, 1885, in Big Flats, N. Y.
566 III. **Sidney Frank,**[10] born Sept. 2, 1889, in Big Flats, N. Y.

---

559 (V) Rose Lottie,[9] daughter of David Russell.[8]

Rose Lottie Tifft, married Nov. 20, 1892, in Big Flats, N.Y., by Rev. H. T. Scholl, to Freeman Leonard.

Residence, Big Flats, N. Y.

CHILD OF ROSE L. AND FREEMAN LEONARD.

567 I. **Russell John,**[10] born July 3, 1895, in Big Flats, N. Y.

---

197 (VII) Nancy V.,[7] daughter of John.[6]

Nancy V. Tifft, married Feb. 2, 1812 to Isaac Dunham, who was born ——— —— ——

Nancy V. Dunham died Nov. 9. 1844.

CHILDREN OF NANCY V. AND ISAAC DUNHAM.

568 I. **Ann V.,**[8] born March 21, 1813, in Stephentown, N. Y.
569 II. **Priscilla,**[8] born ——— ——— in Stephentown, N. Y.
570 III. **Mary T.,**[8] born ——— ——— in Stephentown, N. Y.

568 (I) Ann V.,[8] daughter of Nancy V.[7]

Ann V. Dunham, married May 1, 1834, to Isaiah B. Coleman, who was born in Stephentown, N. Y., May 7, 1809.

Rev. Isaiah Bangs Coleman was the fifth child of Calvin Coleman and the grandson of John Coleman, one of the pioneers of Stephentown. Such advantages as the common schools gave seem to have been the limit of his early education; adding to that, habits of industry and application, he soon qualified himself for teaching, following it for ten years. He experienced religion when eighteen years old. Seven years later he was licensed to preach, and in little less than a year was ordained to the ministry as Free Will Baptist. For nine years he had no settled pastorate. In 1844 he accepted a call to the West Stephentown church, dispensing the Word of Life for forty years among the people there. Not one among those who officiated as clergyman at the marriages of the Rensselaer County Tiffts was so beloved as he.

Not only did he rejoice with them at their wedding feasts, but in times of sorrow and affliction, he mingled his tears with theirs, and gave freely of his loving sympathy. He performed during his pastorate there, three hundred and fifty-three marriage ceremonies, preached four hundred funeral sermons, and in addition, probably preached about five thousand sermons. His tender sympathy was intensified as the years passed, for he went often to the homes in the valleys and on the hillsides to speak words of hope and consolation. He was abundantly blessed with means to further his benevolent intentions (though it is said that he never accepted a stated salary for his services). Nor did he forget the work of Missions, leaving in his will a large sum for its use. He said: "This will help preach the gospel when I am dead."

He entered into rest March 14, 1883.

CHILDREN OF ANN V. AND I. B. COLEMAN.

571 I. **Elbert,**[9] born Dec. 13, 1835, in Stephentown, N. Y.

572 II. **Isaac David,**[9] born Oct. 8, 1837, in Stephentown, N. Y.

571 (I) Elbert,[9] son of Ann V.[8]

Elbert Coleman, married May 31, 1858, in Stephentown, N.Y., to Hannah S. Hollis, and died in Stephentown, Oct. 25, 1878.

CHILDREN OF ELBERT AND HANNAH S. COLEMAN.

573 I. **Florence,**[10] born Feb. 5, 1860, in Stephentown, N. Y.

574 II. **Isaac DeWitt,**[10] born April 11, 1865, in Stephentown, N. Y.

---

573 (I) Florence,[10] daughter of Elbert.[9]

Florence Coleman, married in Stephentown, N. Y., April 3, 1877, to William L. Jackson.

Florence Jackson died in Burnt Hills, N. Y., Nov. 24, 1883.

William L. Jackson died in Burnt Hills, N. Y., June 1, 1893.

---

574 (II) Isaac DeWitt,[10] son of Elbert.[9]

Isaac DeWitt Coleman, married May 11, 1889, in Stephentown, N. Y., to Phebe Saxby.

Isaac DeWitt Coleman, died Nov. 11, 1892, in New York City.

---

572 (II) Isaac David,[9] son of Ann V.[8]

Isaac David Coleman enlisted during the Civil War in the 125th N. Y. S. V., being Orderly Sergeant of Company E. He was afterward promoted, and while leading his men was killed June 16, 1864, in an engagement near Petersburg, Va.

---

572 (II) Priscilla,[8] daughter of Nancy V.[7]

Priscilla Dunham, married William Wheeler. She lived and died in Lebanon, N. Y.

---

570 (III) Mary T.,[8] daughter of Nancy V.[7]

Mary T. Dunham, married Isaiah Barnes.

Isaiah Barnes is dead. Mary T. Barnes resides with son Isaiah in Peatville, Colo.

CHILDREN OF MARY T. AND ISAIAH BARNES.

575 I. **William,**[9] dead.

576 II. **Isaiah.**[9]

---

576 (II) Isaiah,[9] son of Mary T.[8]

Is married and lives in Peatville, Weld Co., Colorado.

---

195 (VIII) Charity,[7] daughter of John.[6]

Charity Tifft, married April 4, 1816, in Nassau, N. Y., to Varnum Maxon Babcock, who was born in Rhode Island, Dec. 26, 1790. He served as Justice of Peace a number of years in Stephentown, N. Y.

Varnum Maxon Babcock died July 15, 1867, at Wagon Landing, Polk County, Wis.

Charity Tifft Babcock died in Stephentown, N. Y., March 2, 1838.

CHILDREN OF CHARITY AND VARNUM M. BABCOCK.

577 I. **John Tifft,**[8] born Dec. 12, 1817, in Nassau, N. Y.

578 II. **Charity,**[8] born Feb. 15, 1820, in Nassau, N. Y.

579 III. **Varnum M., Jr.,**[8] born March 4, 1824, in Nassau, N. Y.

---

577 (I) John Tifft,[8] son of Charity.[7]

John Tifft Babcock died in Alden, N. Y., Feb. 28, 1840.

---

578 (II) Charity,[8] daughter of Charity.[7]

Charity Babcock, married Sept. 16, 1858, in Lyons, N. Y., by Rev. W. A. Fiske, to James Dolby Hunt, who was born in Burlington, Otsego Co., N. Y., Oct. 24, 1812, and died March 12, 1888, at Newark, N. Y.

Charity (Babcock) Hunt resides in Newark, N. Y.

---

579 (III) Varnum Maxon, Jr.,[8] son of Charity.[7]

Varnum Maxon Babcock, Jr., married Sept. 11, 1845, in Stephentown, N. Y., by Rev. R. Collins, to Calista M. Cole, who was born in Nassau, N. Y.

Residence, Amery, Wis.

Varnum M. Babcock, Jr., was a vestryman of St. John's Church; was chairman of the Board of Supervisors of Polk Co., Wis., twelve years; Town Clerk and Assessor two terms; Sheriff one term; Attorney two terms; was appointed by President Cleveland in 1887 Receiver of Public Moneys for the United States Land office at St. Croix Falls; served as chairman of Town Board of Lincoln, Wis., and District Attorney of Polk Co., Wis.; also as Postmaster of Amery, Wis. He drafted the charter for the village of Amery, and took it before the Circuit Court for approval.

CHILDREN OF VARNUM M. AND CALISTA BABCOCK.

580 I. **John Cole,**[9] born July 1, 1846, in Stephentown, N. Y.

581 II. **Charity Tifft,**[9] born Oct. 6, 1860, at Wagon Landing, Wis.

---

580 (I) John Cole,[9] son of Varnum Maxon, Jr.[8]

John Cole Babcock, married Nov. 3, 1869, in Alden, Wis., by Rev. A. B. Peabody, to Sarah E. Dunning, who was born in Ohio.

Residence, Amery, Wis.

581 (11) Charity Tifft,[9] daughter of Varnum Maxon, Jr.[8]

Charity Tifft Babcock, married Sept. 22, 1875, in New Richmond, Wis., by Rev. Mr. Luscum, to Paul Turner.

CHILDREN OF CHARITY T. AND PAUL TURNER.

582 I. **Calista,**[10] born Nov. 6, 1876, in Alden, Wis.
583 II. **Ida,**[10] born Oct. 27, 1878, in Alden, Wis.

---

199 (IX) John, Jr.,[7] son of John.[6]

John Tifft, Jr., married Dec. 24, 1818, to Chloe Field, who was born Jan. 27, 1798, and died April 10, 1864, in Cooper, Mich.

John Tifft, married a second time, April, 13, 1867, to Harriet Joshling, who died Dec. 20, 1869, in Cooper, Mich.

John Tifft died Oct. 20, 1868, in Cooper, Mich.

CHILDREN OF JOHN AND CHLOE TIFFT.

584 I. **Martha Ann,**[8] born Jan. 18, 1820, in Nassau, N. Y.
585 II. **Nancy M.,**[8] born April 3, 1821, in Nassau, N. Y.
586 III. **Sprague Miner,**[8] born April 8, 1823, in Nassau, N.Y.
587 IV. **Spelman V.,**[8] born Jan. 29, 1828, in Nassau, N. Y.
588 V. **Ursula Cabrilla,**[8] born April 28, 1830, in Nassau, N.Y.
589 VI. **Emily Alvira,**[8] born Aug. 6, 1832; died July 14, 1844, in Nassau, N. Y.

---

584 (I) Martha Ann,[8] daughter of John, Jr.[7]

Martha Ann Tifft, married Sept. 6, 1838, in Nassau, N. Y., by Rev. I. B. Coleman, to Isaac J. Hoag, who was born in Chatham, N. Y., March 11, 1819.

Isaac J. Hoag was licensed to preach by the Rensselaer County U. M., in 1846. He was ordained by the Free Will

Baptist Church of Poestenkill, N. Y., Sept. 10, 1848, serving that church six years at that time, and six years again later in life. He was pastor of the Odessa, N. Y. church twice, three years each time, and was in the ministry 43 years. He died in Johnsburgh, Warren Co., N. Y., March 22, 1891. His wife, Martha Ann Tifft Hoag, died in Johnsburgh, N. Y., Dec. 4, 1879.

CHILD OF MARTHA ANN AND ISAAC J. HOAG.

590 I. **Lovina Adell,**[9] born Jan. 12, 1848, in Nassau, N. Y.

---

590 (I) Lovina Adell,[9] daughter of Martha Ann[8]

Lovina Adell Hoag, married Dec. 22, 1869, in Odessa, N. Y., Schuyler Co., by Rev. O. S. Brown, to Joseph Hart Topping, who was born in Montour, N. Y., Sept. 19, 1841, and died in Montour, N. Y., Oct. 12, 1876.

Lovina A. Topping married a second time, March 18, 1879, in Johnsburgh, N. Y., by Rev. I. J. Hoag, to John A. Straight, who was born in Johnsburgh, N. Y., Oct. 12, 1845.

Residence, North Creek, Warren Co., N. Y.

CHILD OF LOVINA A. AND JOSEPH H. TOPPING.

591 I. **Joseph Hoag,**[10] born July 24, 1876, in Montour, N. Y.

CHILDREN OF LOVINA A. AND JOHN A. STRAIGHT.

592 II. **Bennie Eugene,**[10] born Dec. 25, 1879, in Johnsburgh, N. Y.

593 III. **Dema Martha,**[10] born Jan. 14, 1883, in Johnsburgh, N. Y.

594 IV. **Maud Marram,**[10] born July 29, 1889, in Johnsburgh, N. Y.

585 (II) Nancy M,[8] daughter of John, Jr.[7]

Nancy M. Tifft, married Sept. 29, 1838, in Nassau, N. Y., by Rev. A. H. Miller, to Paul Palmer, who was born July 15, 1812, in Nassau, N. Y., and died April 3, 1883, in Alamo, Mich.

CHILD OF NANCY M. AND PAUL PALMER.

595 I. **John H.,**[9] born Aug. 1, 1840, in Nassau, N. Y.

---

595 (I) John H.,[9] son of Nancy M.[8]

John H. Palmer, married March 25, 1868, in Tonawanda, N.Y., to Emily R. Becker.

Residence, Alamo, Mich.

CHILDREN OF JOHN H AND EMILY R. PALMER.

596 I. **Walter H.,**[10] born Dec. 31, 1870, in Alamo, Mich.
597 II. **Charles H.,**[10] born Oct. 19, 1874, in Alamo, Mich.
598 III. **Raymond, A.,**[10] born Feb. 22, 1880, in Alamo, Mich.
599 IV. **Irving J.,**[10] born Jan. 26, 1884, in Alamo, Mich.

---

596 (I) Walter H.,[10] son of John H.[9]

Walter H. Palmer is a teacher in the public schools of Alamo, Mich.

---

597 (II) Charles H.,[10] son of John H.[9]

Charles H. Palmer is in the employ of the Government at Alamo, Mich., as a Postal Clerk.

---

598 (III) Raymond A.,[10] son of John H.[9]

Raymond A. Palmer is a student in the Plainwell, Mich., High School.

---

599 (IV) Irving J.,[10] son of John H.[9]

Irving J. Palmer.

---

586 (IV) Spelman V.,[8] son of John Jr.[7]

Spelman V. Tifft, married Nov. 29, 1845, in Nassau, N. Y., by Rev. I. B. Coleman, to Abigail Wheeler, who was born July 30, 1828, in Nassau, N. Y.

Spelman V. Tifft died Jan. 1, 1895, in Kalamazoo, Mich.

CHILDREN OF SPELMAN V. AND ABIGAIL TIFFT.

600 I. **Melissa,**[9] born May 28, 1847, in Nassau, N. Y.

601 II. **George John,**[9] born March 4, 1852, in Buffalo, N. Y.

602 III. **Edward Spelman,**[9] born Sept. 10, 1854, in Buffalo, N. Y.; died June 19, 1857, in Cooper, Mich.

603 IV. **Carrie Hulda,**[9] born May 5, 1857, in Alamo, Mich.

604 V. **Eugene Montville,**[9] born Jan. 25, 1860, in Alamo, Mich.; died April 8, 1877, in Cooper, Mich.

605 VI. **Francelia Jenette,**[9] born June 15, 1862, in Cooper, Mich.

606 VII. **Etta,**[9] born May 6, 1865, in Cooper, Mich.

607 VIII. **Fred,**[9] born Aug. 23, 1871, in Cooper, Mich.

---

600 (I) Melissa,[9] daughter of Spelman V.[8]

Melissa Tifft, married Jan. 7, 1864, in Cooper, Mich., to Peter Dickerson.

Melissa Dickerson, married a second time Jan. 12, 1876, in Kalamazoo, Mich., to Theodore Armstrong.

CHILD OF MELISSA TIFFT AND PETER DICKERSON.

608 I. **Susan Cora,**[10] born April 20, 1865, in Alamo, Mich.

CHILDREN OF MELISSA AND THEODORE ARMSTRONG.

609 II. **Lewis Darwin,**[10] born Aug. 15, 1877, in Portage, Mich.

610 III. **LaVerne Edson,**[10] born March 20, 1881, in Kalamazoo, Mich.

---

601 (II) George John,[9] son of Spelman V.[8]

George John Tifft, married July 19, 1874, in Alamo, Mich., by J. C. Condon, to Priscilla Weliver.

George John Tifft died Sept. 28, 1888, in Cooper, Mich.

CHILDREN OF GEORGE JOHN AND PRISCILLA TIFFT.

611 I. **Elmer Guy,**[10] born Feb. 14, 1875, in Cooper, Mich.

612 II. **George Fay,**[10] born Oct. 5, 1876, in Portage, Mich.

613 III. **Daisa M.,**[10] born May 18, 1878, in Portage, Mich.

614 IV. **Myrta,**[10] born Jan 8, 1880, in Alamo, Mich.

615 V. **Edna Elvira,**[10] born July 5, 1882, in Alamo, Mich.; died Sept. 4, 1894, in Richland, Mich.

616 VI. **Mabel,**[10] born Sept. 7, 1884, in Cooper, Mich.

---

611 (I) Elmer Guy,[10] son of George John.[9]

Elmer Guy Tifft, married Sept. 11, 1893, in Kalamazoo, Mich., by D. French, J. P., to Nellie C. Deback.

Residence, Kalamazoo, Mich.

---

612 (II) George Fay,[10] son of George John.[9]

George Fay Tifft.

Residence, Kalamazoo, Mich.

---

613 (III) Daisa M.,[10] daughter of George John.[9]

Daisa M. Tifft, married April 19, 1893, in Benton Harbor, Mich., by W. H. Prescott, to Clarence Maddox.

---

614 (IV) Myrta,[10] daughter of George John.[9]

Myrta Tifft.

---

616 (VI) Mabel,[10] daughter of George John[9].

Mabel Tifft.

---

603 (IV) Carrie Hulda,[9] daughter of Spelman V.[8]

Carrie Hulda Tifft, married April, 1873, in Cooper, Mich., by J. Albertson, J. P., to Henry Rogers.

CHILDREN OF CARRIE H. AND HENRY ROGERS.

617 I. **William,**[10] born March 6, 1874, in Cooper, Mich.
618 II. **Delia E.,**[10] born Sept. 3, 1877, in Cooper, Mich.
619 III. **Melinda,**[10] born Nov. 5, 1891, in Scotts, Mich.

---

605 (VI) Francelia Jennette,[9] daughter of Spelman V.[8]

Francelia Jennette Tifft, married Jan. 1, 1878, in Plainwell, Mich, by J. H. Fletcher, to Samuel Mowl.

Residence, Cooper, Mich.

CHILDREN OF FRANCELIA J. AND SAMUEL MOWL.

620 I. **Ora S.,**[10] born Aug. 7, 1880, in Cooper, Mich.
621 II. **Lillie M.,**[10] born Jan. 18, 1883, in Cooper, Mich.

---

606 (VII) Etta,[9] daughter of Spelman V.[8]

Etta Tifft, married Nov. 25, 1879, in Plainwell, Mich. ,by G. L. Cole, to Robert Mowl.

Residence, Kalamazoo, Mich.

CHILDREN OF ETTA AND ROBERT MOWL.

I. **Perley M.,**[10] born Aug. 23, 1881, in Cooper, Mich.
II. **Maud G.,**[10] born March 27, 1884, in Cooper, Mich.
III. **Grace C.,** born March 29, 1889, in Cooper, Mich.

---

607 (VIII) Fred,[9] son of Spelman V.[8]

Fred Tifft, married Nov. 11, 1891, in Kalamazoo, Mich., by J. H. Johnstone, to Effie Bachelder.

Residence, Kalamazoo, Mich.

CHILD OF FRED AND EFFIE TIFFT.

I. **Floyd E.,**[10] born April 16, 1893, in Kalamazoo, Mich.

---

587 (V) Ursula Cabrilla,[8] daughter of John, Jr.[7]

Ursula Cabrilla Tifft, married April 9, 1846, by Rev. I. B. Coleman, to Edward Vickery, who was born Feb. 28, 1826, in Nassau, N. Y., and died Dec. 16, 1880, in Pine Grove, Mich. He served in the Civil War under General McClellan; was in both battles of Bull Run, and was honorably discharged. He was a deacon in the Baptist Church.

Ursula Vickery died May 10, 1870, in Pine Grove, Mich.

CHILDREN OF URSULA C. AND EDWARD VICKERY.

I. **Ira,**[9] born March 8, 1848, in Sand Lake, N Y.
II. **Josiah,**[9] born in 1850.
III. **Emma,**[9] born Aug. 12, 1851, in Sand Lake, N. Y.
IV. **Eli,**[9] born in 1856.

630 V. **Olive,**[9] born in 1864.

631 VI. **Josephine,**[9] born in 1866.

---

626 (I) Ira,[9] son of Ursula Cabrilla.[8]

Ira Vickery was married in 1868, and has held the office of Supervisor three terms.

Residence, Crary, N. Dakota.

CHILDREN OF IRA AND ——— VICKERY.

632 I. **Edwin E.,**[10] born Dec. 28, 1870, Van Buren Co., Mich.

633 II. **Edith M.,**[10] born May 6, 1874.

634 III. **Claud,**[10] born Oct. 6, 1876.

---

627 (II) Josiah,[9] son of Ursula Cabrilla.[8]

Josiah Vickery, married in 1871 and has four children, all church members.

Residence, Kalamazoo, Mich.

CHILDREN OF JOSIAH AND ——— VICKERY.

635 I. **Hannah.**[10]

636 II. **Maime.**[10]

637 III. **Lillie.**[10]

638 IV. **May.**[10]

---

628 (III) Emma,[9] daughter of Ursula Cabrilla.[8]

Emma Vickery, married March 8, 1868 in Pine Grove, Mich., by Esq. Stur, to Mage Milliman, who was born June 4, 1849, in Burns, N. Y.

Married second time in 1880, to Richard T. Scott, in Cooper, Mich.

Residence, Otsego, Mich.

CHILD OF MAGE AND EMMA VICKERY.

639 I. **Rhuel F.,**[10] born April 8, 1869, in Pine Grove, Mich.

---

629 (IV) Eli,[9] son of Ursula Cabrilla.[8]

Eli Vickery, married by Elder Williams. He is a deacon in the Baptist Church.

Residence, Gobles, Mich.

CHILD OF ELI AND ——— VICKERY.

640 I. **Celia.**[10]

---

630 (V) Olive,[9] daughter of Ursula Cabrilla.[8]

Olive Vickery, married in 1889 to Christopher DeLambert. Members of Presbyterian Church.

Residence, Gobles, Mich.

CHILDREN OF OLIVE AND CHRISTOPHER DE LAMBERT.

641 I. ———,[10] died

642 II. **Emma,**[10] born Sept. 17, 1892.

---

631 (VI) Josephine,[9] daughter of Ursula Cabrilla.[8]

Joseph Vickery, married July 2, 1892, in Billings, Montana, by Rev. Mr. Sproule, to Robert L. Davis. Members of Christian Church, Valparaiso, Ind.

Josephine Vickery Davis was educated in the Northern Indiana Normal School, and taught in the public schools of Michigan and Iowa; graduated in Phonography in 1887, and was cashier for two years in the Home Bank, Homeston, Ia.

Residence, Red Lodge, Montana.

CHILD OF JOSEPHINE AND ROBERT L. DAVIS.

643 I. **Glenn,**[10] born Sept. 21, 1893.

---

588 (V) Sprague Miner,[8] son of John, Jr.[7]

Sprague Miner Tifft, married Dec. 23, 1846, in Schodack, N. Y., by Rev. Edward Holmes, to Rebecca Cole, who was born Sept. 16, 1821, in Nassau, N. Y.

Sprague M. Tifft died March 3, 1854.

Rebecca Cole Tifft resides at Malden Bridge, N. Y.

---

200 (X) Sprague,[7] son of John.[6]

Sprague Tifft, married Jan. 10, 1822, in Stephentown, N. Y., to Lydia Culver, (daughter of Levi and Lydia Culver,) who was born in Stephentown, N. Y., in August, 1802, and died March 31, 1823.

Sprague Tifft, married a second time, Oct. 24, 1827, in Caanan, N. Y., by Rev. Z. Clark, to Sophia B. Watson, (daughter of David and Hannah Watson,) who was born in Caanan, March 1, 1809.

Sprague Tifft lived on a portion of the original Tifft Homestead in Nassau, N. Y. He was a remarkable bright old man, retaining all his faculties up to the time of his death, April 28, 1896.

CHILD OF SPRAGUE AND LYDIA TIFFT.

644 I. **Lydia A.,**[8] born Jan. 20, 1823, in Nassau, N. Y.

CHILDREN OF SPRAGUE AND SOPHIA B. TIFFT.

645 II. **Sprague W.,**[8] born Oct. 4, 1829, in Nassau, N. Y.; died Sept. 7, 1831.

646 III. **Arasmus D.,**[8] born Feb. 22, 1830, in Nassau, N. Y.; died March 21, 1830.

647 IV. **George, W.,**[8] born Jan. 29, 1831, in Nassau, N. Y.

648 V. **James Edward,**[8] born Aug. 12, 1832, in Nassau, N.Y.

649 VI. **Willard DeWitt,**[8] born Aug. 13, 1834, in Nassau, N. Y.

650 VII. **Frances S.,**[8] born June 21, 1836, in Nassau, N. Y.

651 VIII. **Cordelia Hannah,**[8] born Sept. 26, 1838, in Nassau, N. Y.

652 IX. **Samuel W.,**[8] born Jan. 24, 1840, in Nassau, N. Y.; died Nov. 17, 1843.

653 X. **Malinda Vallett,**[8] born Aug. 1, 1842, in Nassau, N. Y.

654 XI. **Amelia C.,**[8] born Sept. 25, 1844, in Nassau, N. Y.

655 XII. **Nelson Isaac,**[8] born Dec. 9, 1846, in Nassau, N. Y.

656 XIII. **Martha J.,**[8] born July 23, 1849, in Nassau, N. Y.

657 XIV. **Joseph L.,**[8] born Oct. 21, 1851, in Nassau, N. Y.

658 XV. **Emerson A.,**[8] born Sept. 18, 1853, in Nassau, N. Y.

---

644 (I) Lydia,[8] daughter of Sprague.[7]

Lydia A. Tifft, married June —, 1840, in Troy, N. Y., to Leander O. Daboll, who was born in Stephentown, N. Y., Feb. 4, 1819.

Lydia A. Daboll died in Buffalo, N. Y., Oct. 7, 1868, and was buried in Dunham's Hollow, N. Y.

Leander Daboll was a general merchant for forty years in Dunham's Hollow, and died there Jan. 31, 1892.

CHILDREN OF LYDIA A. AND LEANDER O. DABOLL.

659 I. **George O.,**[9] born April 22, 1841, in Stephentown, N. Y.

660 II. **Willmot C.,**[9] born Oct. 10, 1848, in Stephentown, N. Y.

---

659 (I) George O.,[9] son of Lydia A.[8]

George O. Daboll, married Sept. 12, 1865, by Rev. I. B. Coleman, to Margaret White, who was born in Nassau, N. Y., April 8, 1846.

George O. Daboll was a dealer in general merchandise in Alps, N. Y. He died in Albany, N. Y., April 21, 1895 and buried at Alps, N. Y.

CHILD OF GEORGE O. AND MARGARET DABOLL.

661 I. **Ethelyn S.,**[10] born Feb. 4, 1873, in Nassau, N. Y.

---

660 (II) Willmot C.,[9] son of Lydia A.[8]

Willmot C. Daboll, married Sept. 15, 1869, by Rev. I. B. Coleman, to Sarah Carrier, who was born in Stephentown, N. Y., Oct. 5, 1850, and died June 27, 1872.

Willmot C. Daboll, married a second time, Sept. 29, 1875, by Rev. I. B. Coleman, to Sarah E. Kelly, who was born in Troy, N. Y., Jan. 28, 1852.

Wilmot C. Daboll is the manager of R. G. Dunn's Mercantile Agency in Troy, N. Y.

CHILD OF WILLMOT C. AND SARAH DABOLL.

662 I. **George W.,**[10] born July 22, 1871, in Nassau, N. Y.

CHILD OF WILLMOT C. AND SARAH E. K. DABOLL.

663 II. **Helena A.,**[10] born Sept. 15, 1878, in Troy, N. Y.

---

662 (I) George W.,[10] son of Willmot C.[9]

George W. Daboll is employed in the Saving Department of National State Bank of Troy, N. Y.

---

647 (IV) George W.,[8] son of Sprague.[7]

George W. Tifft, married Oct. 7, 1852, in Albany, N. Y., by Rev. H. Washburn, to Julia A. Larkin, who was born May 6, 1831, in Nassau, N. Y.

Residence, 727 River St., Troy, N. Y.

CHILDREN OF GEORGE W. AND JULIA A. TIFFT.

664 I. **Georgianna L.,**[9] born March 4, 1854, in Halfmoon, N. Y.; died May 4, 1875.

665 II. **Flora E.,**[9] born Aug. 4, 1856.
666 III. **Carrie E.,**[9] born Aug. 22, 1866.
667 IV. **Grace B.,**[9] born Oct. 21, 1872.

665 (II) Flora E.,[9] daughter of George W.[8]

Flora E. Tifft, married April 9, 1879, in Clifton Park, N. Y., by Rev. Mr. Howe, to Richard Hill, who was born in New York City, Feb. 27, 1857.

666 (III) Carrie E.,[9] daughter of George W.[8]

Carrie E. Tifft, married Oct. 21, 1891, in Halfmoon, N. Y., by Rev. Mr. Allen, to Charles Englemore, who was born April 23, 1866, in Clifton Park, N. Y.

667 (IV) Grace B.,[9] daughter of George W.[8]

Grace B. Tifft.

648 (V) James Edward,[8] son of Sprague.[7]

James Edward Tifft, married Sept. 15, 1857, in Nassau, N. Y., by Rev. N. Van Alstine, to Mary Ann Weir, who was born in Nassau, N. Y., April 10, 1835, and died July 21, 1860.

James E. Tifft, married a second time, March 12, 1871, to Carrie E. Sickles.

He enlisted Aug. 15, 1861 in the 125th N. Y. V., Co. E, for three years, and was discharged June 5, 1864, at Alexandria, Va.

James E. Tifft died in Troy, N. Y., June 15, 1874.

CHILD OF JAMES EDWARD AND MARY ANN TIFFT.

668 I. **Alice A.,**[9] born July 11, 1858 in Stephentown, N. Y.

CHILD OF JAMES EDWARD AND CARRIE E. TIFFT.

669 II. **Edward S.,**[9] born June 8, 1873, in Troy, N. Y.

---

668 (I) Alice A.,[9] daughter of James Edward.[8]

Alice A. Tifft, married Dec. 23, to John Hitchcock, who was born Nov. 15, 1853, in West Hawley, Mass.

Residence, Hoag's Corners, N. Y.

CHILDREN OF ALICE A. AND JOHN HITCHCOCK.

670 I. **Edward S.,**[10] born May 13, 1881.

671 II. **Malinda L.,**[10] born May 4, 1883.

---

669 (II) Edward S.,[9] son of James Edward.[8]

Edward S. Tifft.

---

649 (VI) Willard DeWitt,[8] son of Sprague.[7]

Willard DeWitt Tifft, married July 4, 1864, in Crooked Lake, N. Y., by Rev. I. B. Coleman, to Adaline S. Larkin, who was born in Nassau, N. Y., Nov. 2, 1840.

Willard DeWitt Tifft has been Postmaster at Hoag's Corners, N. Y., for twenty years.

Residence, Hoag's Corners, N. Y.

CHILDREN OF WILLARD DEWITT AND ADALINE S. TIFFT.

672 I. **Winnie M.,**[9] born Nov. 6, 1866, in Nassau, N. Y.

673 II. **Delmar D.,**[9] born Jan. 29, 1870, in Nassau, N. Y.; died Nov. 15, 1890 in Hoag's Corners, N. Y.

674 III. **Charles S.,**[9] born July 28, 1873, in Nassau, N. Y.

675 IV. **Jennie A.,**[9] born July 4, 1875. in Hoag's Corners, Y. Y.

676 V. **Mabel F.,**[9] born July 24, 1881, in Hoag's Corners, N. Y.

677 VI. **Florence A.,**[9] born Oct. 9, 1883, in Hoag's Corners, N.Y.

---

672 (I) Winnie M.,[9] daughter of Willard DeWitt.[8]

Winnie M. Tifft, married June 13, 1887, in Hoag's Corners, N. Y., by Rev. P. L. Dow, to James M. Adsit, who was born in Clifton Park, N. Y., Sept. 18, 1866.

---

674 (III) Charles S.,[9] son of Willard DeWitt.[8]

Charles S. Tifft, married July 14, 1894, in Sand Lake, N. Y., by Rev. R. Washburn, to Hattie M. Adams, who was born in Sand Lake, July 22, 1878.

---

675 (IV) Jennie A.,[9] daughter of Willard DeWitt.[8]

Jennie A. Tifft.

---

676 (V) Mabel F.,[9] daughter of Millard DeWitt.[8]

Mabel F. Tifft.

---

677 (VI) Florence A.,[9] daughter of Willard DeWitt.[8]

Florence A. Tifft.

---

650 (VII.) Frances S.,[8] daughter of Sprague.[7]

Frances S. Tifft, married Sept. 9, 1856, in Nassau, N. Y., by Rev. I. B. Coleman, to Charles S. White, who was born in Nassau, N. Y., Sept. 5, 1833.

Residence, Newark, N. Y.

CHILD OF FRANCES S. AND CHARLES S. WHITE.

678 I. **Fred C.,**[9] born July 1, 1858, in Nassau, N. Y.

---

678 (I) Fred C.,[9] son of Frances S.[8]

Fred C. White, married Oct. 11, 1882, in Newark, N. Y., by J. H. Moore, to Minnie May Horton, who was born in Arcadia, N. Y.

Residence, Newark, N. Y.

CHILD OF FRED C. AND MINNIE M. WHITE.

679 I. **Elmer F.,**[10] born Dec. 24, 1883, in Newark, N. Y.

---

651 (VIII) Cordelia Hannah,[8] daughter of Sprague.[7]

Cordelia Hannah Tifft, married Dec. 31, 1860, in Nassau, N. Y., by Rev. I. B. Coleman, to Eugene E. Gardner, who was born in Stephentown, N. Y., March 4, 1836.

In 1863 E. E. Gardner moved to Phelps, Ontario Co., N. Y., and in partnership with Mr. Cornell, bought and operated the Ontario Flouring Mills. They sold the mills in 1867 and bought a farm at East Newark.

Cordelia H. Gardner was a member of Ontario Grange and edited the Grange paper.

She died Sept. 17, 1887, in East Newark, N. Y.

CHILD OF CORDELIA H. AND EUGENE E. GARDNER.

670 I. **Pearl S.,**[9] born, Nov. 4, 1866, in Phelps, N. Y.

---

680 (I) Pearl S.,[9] daughter of Cordelia.[8]

Pearl S Gardner, married March 26, 1889, in Clyde, N. Y., by Rev. J. B. Vrooman, to Edward Parkhurst, who was born in Ashford, Kent Co., England, Feb. 4, 1864.

Residence, Newark, N. Y.

CHILD OF PEARL S. AND EDWARD PARKHURST.

681 I. **Malcolm Earl,**[10] born May 24, 1890; died Sept. 16, 1890, in Newark, N. Y.

653 (X) Malinda Vallett,[8] daughter of Sprague.[7]

Malinda Vallett Tifft, married Sept. 30, 1870, in Hoag's Corner's N. Y., by Rev. I. B. Coleman, to Jedadiah Chatman, who was born in Stephentown, N. Y., Aug. 30, 1834.

Residence, Hoag's Corners, N. Y.

654 (XI) Amelia C.,[8] daughter of Sprague.[7]

Amelia C. Tifft resides with her aged parents on the homestead, Nassau, N. Y.

655 (XII) Nelson Isaac,[8] son of Sprague.[7]

Nelson Isaac Tifft, married Feb. 2, 1870, in Nassau, N. Y., by Rev. I. B. Coleman, to Frances Mary Larkin, who was born June 17, 1848, in Nassau, N. Y.

Residence, Hoag's Corners, N. Y.

CHILD OF NELSON ISAAC AND FRANCES M. TIFFT.

682 I. **Bertha May,**[9] born Aug. 17, 1882, in Hoag's Corners.

656 (XIII) Martha J.,[8] daughter of Sprague.[7]

Martha J. Tifft, married March 27, 1873, in Nassau, N. Y., by Rev. I. B. Coleman, to Isaiah Johnson, who was born in 1845, in West Stephentown, N. Y.

Residence, East Greenbush, N. Y.

CHILDREN OF MARTHA J. AND ISAIAH JOHNSON.

683 I. **Martha Sophia,**[9] born Jan. 21, 1874, in Nassau, N. Y.

684 II. **Frederick A.,**[9] born June 22, 1879, in Nassau, N. Y.

685 III. **Sprague V.,**[9] born March 17, 1882, in Nassau, N. Y.

686 IV. **Melvina S.,**[9] born July 25, 1883, in Nassau, N. Y.

683 (I) Martha Sophia,[9] daughter of Martha J.[8]

Martha Sophia Johnson, married April 5, 1889, in Spring Lake, N. Y., by Rev. D. P. Frink, to Charles Fuller, who was born in Conquest, N. Y., July 13, 1870.

CHILD OF MARTHA SOPHIA AND CHARLES FULLER.

687 I. **Melvina J.,**[10] born June 4, 1892, in Spring Lake, N. Y.

---

657 (XIV) Joseph L.,[8] son of Sprague.[7]

Joseph L. Tifft, married Dec. 31, 1885, in Troy, N. Y., by Rev. Dr. Dow, to Lillie Bolles, who was born in Troy, N. Y., March 24, 1866.

Residence, Troy, N. Y.

CHILD OF JOSEPH L. AND LILLIE TIFFT.

688 I. **Ella May,**[9] born Feb. 2, 1888; died Nov. 25, 1892.

---

658 (XV) Emerson A.,[8] son of Sprague.[7]

Emerson A. Tifft, married May 28, 1887, in Belford, Mich., by Rev. Charles Evans, to Anna B. Tiffany, who was born in Phelps, N. Y., Oct. 21, 1859.

Residence, 2206 W. Monroe St., Chicago, Ill.

---

201 (XI) Joseph,[7] son of John.[6]

Joseph Tifft, married Dec. 3, 1825, in Sand Lake, N. Y., by Marcus Peck, J. P., to Sally Cross Simmons, who was born Oct. 5, 1803.

Joseph Tifft lived on half of the original Tifft Homestead in Nassau, N. Y., which consisted of two hundred acres. After his father's death, Joseph and Sprague cared for their mother (Anna).

Joseph Tefft died in Nassau, N. Y., May 24, 1879.

Sally C. Tifft died in Nassau, March 23, 1885.

689 I. **Abbie Jane,**[8] born Oct. 21, 1826, in Nassau, N. Y.; died Feb. 24, 1828, in Nassau, N. Y.

690 II. **Joseph Cyrus,**[8] born Jan. 28, 1828, in Nassau, N. Y.; died Oct. 29, 1840, in Nassau, N. Y.

691 III. **Abigail Simmons,**[8] born April 26, 1833, in Nassau, N. Y.

692 IV. **Susan Ann,**[8] born June 10, 1835, in Nassau, N. Y.

693 V. **Ulissa M.,**[8] born April 22, 1837 in Nassau, N. Y.; died April, 6, 1839.

694 VI. **Sarah Maria,**[8] born Nov. 9, 1844, in Nassau, N. Y.

695 VII. **Charity Matilda,**[8] born Aug. 19, 1845, in Nassau, N. Y.; died July 13, 1847.

---

691 (III) Abigail Simmons,[7] daughter of Joseph[6]

Abigail Simmons Tifft, married Jan. 28, 1866, in Nassau, N. Y., by. Rev. I. B. Coleman, to Zachariah Smith. (Separated.)

Residence, North Nassau, N. Y.

---

692 (IV) Susan Ann,[8] daughter of Joseph.[7]

Susan Ann Tifft, married Feb. 29, 1860, in Nassau, N. Y., by Rev. I. B. Coleman, to Stephen Edgar Williams, who was born July 7, 1834.

Residence, North Nassau, N. Y.

---

694 (VI) Sarah Maria,[8] daughter of Joseph.[7]

Sarah Maria Tifft, married Sept. 5, 1870, in Nassau, N. Y., by Rev. I. B. Coleman, to George Giles, and died in Nassau, N. Y., Aug. 12, 1877.

---

202 (XII) George Washington,[7] son of John.[6]

George Washington Tifft, married March 14, 1827, to Lucy Enos, the daughter of Joseph and Thankful Enos, who was born Dec. 2, 1805, in New Lebanon, N. Y., and died Aug. 21, 1870, in Buffalo, N. Y.

George Washington Tifft's first business enterprise was the clearing of timber land in the vicinity of his early home. This, with other similar ventures, combined with his natural business sagacity, resulted in his having, when 21 years of age, quite a sum of money for that locality. He remained in Nassau, N. Y., after his marriage until he was 25 years of age, at which time he removed to his farm, previously purchased, in Orleans County. In 1841 he went to Michigan City, Ind., and engaged in buying and shipping grain. In 1842 he came to Buffalo and formed a co-partnership with the late Dean Richmond in the milling business, and in 1843 he opened a branch of the transportation line, known as the Troy and Michigan Six-day Line,—(did not run on Sundays), under the name of George W. Tifft & Co. Selling his interest in the boats the next year, he formed a partnership with Henry H. Sizer in the produce and commission business. For the nine years following this he gave his attention to the milling business. He was prominent among the founders of the International Bank of Buffalo, of which he was the first president, occupying the position until 1857, the year of the great financial crash, which carried down so many banks and business houses. He among others was compelled to suspend.

In 1857 he took hold of the steam engine company, built blast furnaces and conceived the idea of smelting Lake Superior ore with mineral coal. In 1858 Mr. Tifft became the president of the New York & Lake Erie Railroad. About this time he turned his attention to the improvement of real estate and became an extensive builder, putting up the Tifft House, Buffalo, then the principal hotel of the city; also the Tifft elevator, besides about 74 dwelling houses. Soon after he came to Buffalo he purchased about 600 acres of land in the southern portion of the city, known as the Tifft Farm. This tract he sold, with the

exception of a few parcels which he disposed of to his children. He also owned an extensive tract of land in Shelby County, Iowa.

The last twenty years of his life was given chiefly to the management of the Buffalo Engine Works, which was owned by the firm of George W. Tifft, Sons & Co.

Amid all the changes of his eventful life Mr. Tifft always maintained an unimpaired credit; always holding his obligations sacred. He took a deep interest in public affairs, although never accepting office. He was a great admirer of Lincoln and gave largely toward the support of the war.

During the whole of his residence in Buffalo, a period of 40 years, he was identified with the Central Presbyterian Church. George W. Tifft died June 24, 1882, in Buffalo, N. Y.

CHILDREN OF GEORGE WASHINGTON AND LUCY TIFFT.

696 I. **John Vallett,**[8] born March 28, 1828, in Stephentown, N. Y.

697 II. **Sarah Ann,**[8] born Oct. 25, 1829, in Stephentown, N. Y.

698 III. **Lucy,**[8] born April 10, 1837, in Hulburton, N. Y.

699 IV. **George Harrison,**[8] born April 13, 1840, in Holly, N.Y.

700 V. **Mary Augusta,**[8] born June 24, 1843, in Holly, N. Y.

696 (I) John Vallett,[8] son of George Washington.[7]

John Vallett Tifft, married April 17, 1882, in Buffalo, by Rev. David Frazer, to Maria L. Pitkin.

John Vallett Tifft died Jan. 3, 1884, in Buffalo, N. Y.

Maria L. Tifft resides in Buffalo, N. Y.

697 (II) Sarah Ann,[8] daughter of George Washington[7]

Sarah Ann Tifft, married Jan. 11, 1854, in Buffalo, N. Y., by Rev. John C. Lord, D. D., to Charles C. F. Gay, M. D., who

was born in Pittsfield, Mass., Jan. 7, 1821, (the son of William and Maria Gay,) and died March 17, 1886, in Buffalo, N, Y.

Dr. Gay was a skillful surgeon, and was connected with the General Hospital of Buffalo, N. Y., for more than twenty years. He was also Professor of Surgery in the Medical Department of Niagara University of Buffalo for a number of years. He was one of the founders of the Society of Natural Sciences and a member of the original board of directors. Was also, for many years, connected with the State Medical Society, and with the Erie County Medical Society, of which he was president for some time.

Mrs. S. A. Gay is one of the corporate managers of the "Home for the Friendless" in Buffalo, representing the Central Presbyterian Church.

ADOPTED CHILD OF SARAH ANN AND DR. C. C. F. GAY.

702 II. **Louis Whiting,**[9] born Feb. 18, 1869, in Buffalo, N. Y.

---

698 (III) Lucy,[8] daughter of George Washington.[7].

Lucy Tifft, married Dec. 2, 1863, in Buffalo, N. Y., by Rev. John C. Lord, D. D., to Charles L. Whiting of Brooklyn, N. Y., and died Feb. 27, 1869, in Buffalo, N. Y.

She was graduated with honor when 16 years of age, from the Buffalo Female Seminary. She received the gold medal as the best mathematician of the school. Professor Davies, author of Davies' Algebra and Geometry, spoke of her ability upon that occasion in high terms.

CHILDREN OF LUCY AND CHARLES L. WHITING.

701 I. **George W. Tifft,**[9] born Feb. 8, 1866, in Buffalo, N. Y.; died Dec. 3, 1876.

702 II. **Louis,**[9] born Feb. 18, 1869, in Buffalo, N. Y.

702 (II) Louis Whiting,[9] son of Lucy,[8] and adopted son of Dr. C. C. F. and Sarah A. Gay.

Louis Whiting Gay, married Aug. 31, 1886, in Tonawanda, N. Y., by Rev. J. P. Smith, to Gertrude Cornell, who was born in Oil City, Pa., Dec. 8, 1871.

---

699 (IV) George Harrison,[8] son of George Washington.[7]

George Harrison Tifft was killed by a falling wall at the burning of the American Hotel at Buffalo, N. Y., Jan. 25, 1865, while serving as fireman in the Citizens Taylor Hose Company No. 1.

---

700 (V) Mary Augusta,[8] daughter of George Washington.[7]

Mary Augusta Tifft, married Sept. 5, 1865, in Buffalo, N. Y., N. Y., by Rev. John C. Lord, D. D., to George D. Plympton, who was born in Buffalo, May, 1839, and died Nov., 1890, in Buffalo, N. Y.

Mary Augusta Plympton was graduated when 16 years of age from Buffalo Female Seminary. She belongs to the Graduates' Association of the same school, and is also a member of the Woman's Twentieth Century Club.

CHILDREN OF MARY A. AND GEORGE D. PLYMPTON.

703 I. **Lucy Tifft,**[9] born June 26, 1868, in Buffalo, N. Y.

704 II. **Alice Gardner,**[9] born Oct. 14, 1870, in Buffalo, N. Y.

704 (II) Alice Gardner,[9] daughter of Mary Augusta.[8]

Alice Gardner Plympton, married June 28, 1892, in Buffalo, N. Y., by Rev. S. S. Mitchell, D. D., to Peter C. Cornell, M. D., who was born in Buffalo, June 28, 1865.

APPENDIX A.

State of Rhode Island,

Secretary of State's Office, Providence.

APRIL 26, 1895.

MRS. MARIA E. TIFFT, Buffalo, N. Y.

Madam:—In reply to yours of the 22nd would say that your former communication was received and have just been able to make the search for information desired. I find the name as follows:

Tefft.	**Teft.**	**Tifft.**	**Tift.**
Abraham.	Daniel.	Caleb.	David.
Gardner.	James.	Daniel.	Samuel, Jr.
James.	John.	David.	
Robert.		David, Sr.	
Solomon.		George.	
		Oliver.	
		Robert.	
		Solomon.	
		Thomas.	

The above named persons served in the Revolutionary War, as appears of record in this office.

Yours respectfully,

C. P. BENNETT,

Sec. of State.

State of Rhode Island,
Secretary of State's Office, Providence.

October 7, 1895.

Mrs. Maria E. Tifft, Buffalo, N. Y.

Madam:—In reply to yours of October 2nd would say, I think John and Robert Tefft came from the town of Richmond in this state, as I learn from the records of that town, that

John Tefft was born in Richmond, March 9, 1729.

Robert Tefft was born in Richmond, May 25, 1732.

The name is spelled Tefft all through said town records. The spelling in our Revolutionary records is very bad, and is undoubtedly due to the scribe's inability to spell correctly.

Yours respectfully,

C. P. BENNETT,

Sec. of State.

State of Rhode Island,
Secretary of State's Office, Providence.

September, 30, 1895.

I hereby certify that it appears of record in this office that John Teft served as a private in Captain Jesse Burdick's Company of militia, being a detachment from Col. Joseph Noye's regiment, from Nov. 7 to Dec. 5, 1777, being ordered on duty by the General Assembly.

Attest. CHARLES P. BENNETT,

[SEAL] Sec. of State.

September, 30, 1895.

I hereby certify that it appears of record in this office that Robert Tifft served in the Revolutionary War as a Corporal in Captain Samuel Gorton's company, under the command of Caleb Lewis Teft, ordered on duty Dec. 21, 1777, and served to January 20, 1778; also that Robert Teft enlisted in Capt. Benjamin West's company in Col. Topham's regiment March 12,

1778; also that Robert Tefft served as a private in Capt. Benjamin West's company in Col. John Topham's regiment from July 16, 1778; also that Robert Tift served as a private in Capt. Benjamin West's company in Col. Topham's regiment from Jan. 16 to March 16, 1779.

Attest: CHARLES P. BENNETT,

[SEAL] Sec. of State.

There appears in the New York State Archives the following names of Revolutionary soldiers:

Nathaniel Tifft, private, Van Woert, Regiment, Wells Co.
Stanton Tifft, private, Van Woert, Regiment, Wells Co.
Stanton Tifft, private, Van Woert, Regiment, Wells Co.

APPENDIX B.

MISCELLANEOUS.

From the Vital Records of Rhode Island.

Jane Tefft, married George Gardiner Sept. 1, 1744.

Sarah Tefft, married in the Sabbatharian Church, Newport, R. I., Sept. 17, 1679.

William Tefft, of Pawtucket and Ruth Vaughn of Cumberland, married by Elder James Wilson in Providence, Aug. 19, 1835.

Thomas Tefft and Abby Millard, married by Rev. Stephen Gano, Nov, 27, 1808.

Daniel Tefft and Experience Millard, married Dec. 2, 1813, Providence.

Abby Tefft and Charles Holbrook, married Sept. 1, 1842, by Elder J. A. McKensie.

John Tefft and Sarah Aman, married Jan. 22, 1797, by Rev. Gardiner Thurston.

From South Kingstown Records.

Joanna Tefft and John Webb, married April 28, 1721.

Samuel, of John, and Mary Barber, married Oct. 1, 1727, by Rouse Helme, assistant.

Stephen Tefft and Annie Gardiner, married Dec. 10, 1742, by Isaac Shelden.

Ebenezer Tefft and Lydia Swift married by Isaac Sheldon, Justice, Nov. 6, 1746.

Mercy Tefft and Thomas Miller of Dighton, Mass., married Dec. 1, 1756.

Mary Tefft and Jeremiah Albro, married Oct. 15, 1758.

Mary Tefft and Henry Joslin, married May 21, 1769.

Abigail Tefft, daughter of Ebenezer, and James Gardiner, married June 27, 1771.

James Tefft, Jr., and Mary Wescott, married Feb. 6, 1772, by T. Perry, Justice.

Mary Tefft, daughter of George, and William Cottrell, married Dec. 7, 1786.

Daniel Tefft and Sarah Northrup, married Feb. 9, 1765, by Samuel Helme, Justice.

Susan C. Tefft, of South Kingstown, and William Davis of Fall River, Mass., married Dec. 9, 1849.

Lyndon G. Tefft, son of Eligah and Frances, and Anna Champlain, daughter of Robert and Esther Champlain, married Aug. 18, 1845, by Thomas Vernon.

Amie Tefft daughter of Eligah and Frances, and Benjamin G. Tefft, of Augustus and Frances, married Nov. 28, 1844.

Mary Ann Tefft and James A. Nicols, married March 11, 1849.

Stephen Hazard Tefft, son of Stephen and Mary B., of North Kingstown, and Phebe Weedon, daughter of Freeman P. and Phebe Watson, of South Kingstown, married Jan. 23, 1849 at Lonsdale, R. I., by Rev. E. T. Watson.

Stephen A. Tefft, son of Benjamin, of Richmond, and Eunice A. daughter of Arnold Lewis, of Exeter, married June 20, 1850, by Rev. George K. Clarke.

Births of the Tefft Family Recorded in South Kingstown.

Ebenezer, born Feb. 14, 1723-4.

Abigail, of Samuel and Joanna, born Dec. 4, 1731.

Mary, born Jan. 28, 1732.

Mercy, born April 24, 1735.
Hannah, of Tennant and Tabitha, born June 28, 1741.
Caleb, born Oct. 11, 1743.
Sophia, of Samuel, Jr., and Mary.
Samuel, born June 22, 1742.
Oliver, born March 22, 1743.
Alexander, born July 30, 1746.
Stanton, of Nathan and Isabel, born July 9, 1744.
Isabel, born March 14, 1745.
Mercy, born Dec. 14, 1749.
Nathan, born Aug. 28, 1752.
John, born March 24, 1756.
Mary, born May 2, 1758.
Sarah, born Aug. 14, 1762.

Marriages Recorded in Exeter.

Mary Tefft and William Hesaline, married June 4, 1787.
Mrs. Patience Tefft and Wilcox Barber, married June, 1797.
Mercy Tefft and John Reynolds, married June 4, 1804.
George Tefft, of Exeter, and Alice James of Richmond, daughter of Stephen James, married April 1, 1827, by Gershom Palmer.
Alice Tefft and Amos Tefft, married Dec. 29, 1839, by Elder Benedict Johnson.

Marriages Recorded in Westerly.

David Tefft and Freelove Palmilter, married Nov. 26, 1737, by Elder John Maxson.
Sarah Tefft and Thomas Wilcox, married July 2, 1739.
Samuel Tefft, of Westerly, and Mary Ellis of Preston, Conn , married at Stonington, Conn., May 5, 1753; by Simeon Miner, Justice.
Mary Tefft and Benajah Brown, married Jan. 25, 1758.
Mary Tefft and Joseph Bundy, married Oct. 31, 1758.

Samuel Tefft, of Westerly, and Elizabeth Mitchell, a widowed daughter of Joseph Bundy, married July 25, 1767, by Rev. Thomas Ross.

Elizabeth Tefft and Thomas Partelow, married April 29, 1784.

Records of Richmond.

Ezekiel Tefft, of Richmond and Patience Porter of Exeter, married Oct. 21, 1750, by Stephen Richmond, Justice.

Ruth Tefft and William Clarke, married March 30, 1737.

Joseph Tefft, Jr., and Sarah Maxson, married July 17, 1757, by Edward Perry, Justice.

Esther Tefft and Oliver Colgrave, married April 28, 1765.

Elizabeth Tefft and Stephen Hoxsie, married Oct. 12, 1766.

Samuel Tefft, son of Joseph, and Amie Gardiner, daughter of George, married Dec. 9, 1770, by Robert Stanton, Justice.

Joseph Tefft, Jr., of Richmond, and Alice, daughter of Samuel Albro, of Exeter, married May 22, 1771, at Exeter, by Elder Solomon Sprague.

Hezekiah Tefft, son of Ezekiel, and Sarah Lillibridge, daughter of Edward, married March 23, 1775, by Edward Perry, Justice.

Tabor Tefft, son of Joseph, and Sarah Barber, daughter of Caleb, married July 25, 1782, by Elder Charles Boss.

Ezekiel Tefft, son of Ezekiel and Amie Wilcox, daughter of Stephen, married Oct. 13, 1783, by Thomas Tefft, Justice.

Sarah Tefft married Benjamin Barber, Oct, 16, 1785.

Susannah Tefft and Lawton Foster, married Nov. 4, 1792.

Mary Tefft married John Reynolds, June 24, 1804.

Edward Tefft, of Richmond, and Nancy Turner, of Groton, Conn., married by Elder John G. Weightman, Dec. 16, 1804.

Lucy Tefft, daughter of George, of Borton, Conn., and Thomas Tefft, Jr., married Jan. 30, 1805.

Sarah Tefft and Luke Clarke, married Feb. 28, 1806.

Joanna Tefft and Joseph Clarke, married Dec. 10, 1810.

Sarah Tefft and John Barber, married Feb. 2, 1826.

Ray G. Tifft, of Richmond, and Mrs. Mary Smith, of South Kingstown, married by Elder Henry C. Hubbard, Sept. 24. 1826.

Deborah Tefft and John Barber, married Dec. 27, 1847.

Silas W. Tefft, son of Silas, of Richmond, and Sarah Crandall daughter of Stephen, married by Elder C. J. Locke, Dec. 27, 1847.

Births of the Tefft Family Recorded in Richmond.

Reynolds, son of John, Jr., and Hannah, born Oct. 6, 1752; died July 5, 1754.

Clarke, born Jan. 7, 1761.

John, born May 18, 1767.

Mary, born April 22, 1769.

Caleb, son of Joseph, Jr., and Sarah, born Oct. 17, 1757.

Mary, born Nov. 24, 1758.

Tabor, born March 3, 1761.

Jemima, born July 10, 1763.

Joseph, born April 6, 1766.

Sarah, born June 12, 1768.

Anotice, born April 1, 1773.

Alice, born June 16, 1775.

Albro, born Sept. 27, 1778.

Phebe Woodmansee, daughter of Penelope, born Jan. 3, 1765.

Joanna, daughter of Benjamin and Deborah, born Feb. 7, 1766.

Edward, born March 12, 1768.

Elizabeth, born Sept. 10, 1770.

Asa, born June 2, 1772.

Jesse, born April 21, 1776.

John Tift (one authority calls him George) must have been an early settler of Stephentown, N. Y., as his daughter Rhoda married Griswald Denison, the son of Daniel Denison, Jr., the settler of 1771. Rhoda's second marriage was to James Jones. It occurred when she and her husband were between 70 and 75 years of age. James Jones died in Stephentown, N. Y., 1885, aged 93

years, and she died some years previous. Rhoda had a brother, John Tifft, who married, had four sons and one daughter, and settled on a farm in Scipio, Cayuga Co., N. Y.

Parker W. Tefft, of Chicago, Ill., gives the following concerning his family:

Edmund Tefft (great-grandfather of Parker W.,) was born in South Kingstown, Kings Co., R. I., Aug. 11, 1750. He was a Baptist preacher and was a volunteer in the Revolutionary War. His father's name is not known. Edmund settled in New York, probably in Rensselaer County, prior to the Revolution, as his son, John Tefft, was born in Stephentown, N. Y., June 28, 1775. Edmund married Mary Sweet, who was born in Exeter, R. I.

From **William Carleton Tifft,** of Marion, N.Y., the following concerning his family is given. He says:

"We know that *our* family at first had only one 'f' in the name."

Caleb Tifft (great-grandfather of William Carleton) was born in Rhode Island. He lived for a long time in Lorraine, Jefferson Co., N. Y., and is buried at Pierrepont Manor, Jefferson Co., N. Y.

Caleb's brothers settled in Saratoga Co., N. Y., where there are now many Teffts or Tiffts.

CHILDREN OF CALEB TEFFT.

Caleb, Jr.,
Stephen,
John,
Barton,
Henry,
Thomas.

Thomas Tifft's wife, up to a year or two ago, was still living with her daughter, Mrs. Dr. Siass, Ellis Village, Jefferson County, N. Y., at the age of 93. She has taken great pride in the collection of her husband's family records.

CALEB, JR., SON OF CALEB.

Caleb Tifft, Jr., lived in Mansville, N. Y., or in Sandy Creek, Oswego, Co., N. Y.

CHILDREN OF CALEB TIFFT, JR.

Orange Angell,
William Theodore,
Daniel, (deceased) of Lacona, Oswego Co., N. Y.
Leander, (deceased) of Pulaski, N. Y.

Orange Angell Tifft always said that his grandfather Caleb had three brothers.

SON OF ORANGE ANGELL TIFFT.

William Carleton Tifft, a graduate of Rochester University and member of the Alpha Delta Phi College Fraternity. Principal of Marion Collegiate Institute, Marion, N. Y.

SON OF DANIEL TIFFT.

William Brainard Tifft of Syracuse, N. Y.

SONS OF LEANDER TIFFT.

Wilbor S. Tifft, of Sandy Creek, N. Y.
Warren H. Tifft, of Sandy Creek, N. Y.

APPENDIX C.

Organization of the Tifft Family Cemetery Association

GARFIELD, N. Y., Oct. 21, 1895.

MRS. W. S. TIFFT, Buffalo, N. Y.

Dear Friend:—Yours of the 13th inst. received, and in reply to your inquiry will say, the name by which we unanimously decided to become incorporated was "The Tifft Cemetery Association," which was organized the 14th day of June, 1882, at the residence of Joseph Tifft, deceased. There were present:

Mrs. Sally C. Tifft, Sprague Tifft and wife, Stephen E. Williams and wife, Willard D. Tifft, Charles Wicks and wife, M. J. Lester and wife, Mrs. Abigail Smith, John R. Knapen of Nussau, N. Y., Jeremiah V. Tifft of Stephentown, N. Y., David Tifft of New Lebanon, N. Y., Wrilson S. Tifft and wife and Mrs. Lily Lord Tifft, of Buffalo, N. Y., and Mrs. Cordelia Gardner of Newark, N. Y.

It was incorporated under the laws of the State of New York, authorizing the incorporation of Family Cemetery Associations. Certificate made out, signed and acknowledged the 17th day of June, and recorded in the office of the County Clerk the 30th day of June, in Book No. 1 of Certificates, at page 74.

Respectfully,

JOHN R. KNAPEN, Clerk.

The cemetery is situated on the Tifft Homestead, Nassau, N. Y. A memorial stone was erected there in May, 1895, by the grandchildren of John Tifft, with the following inscriptions engraved upon the four faces:

Front.

JOHN TIFFT
BORN IN EXETER, R. I.,
FEB. 19, 1758.
DIED IN NASSAU, N. Y., APRIL 26, 1813.

ANNA VALLETT.
HIS WIFE.
BORN IN NORTH KINGSTOWN, R. I.,
FEBRUARY 13, 1760.
DIED IN NASSAU, N. Y., MARCH 23, 1834.

Back.

ROBERT, born, Exeter, R.I., 1779; died, Stephentown, N.Y., 1860.
ABIGAIL, born, Exeter, R.I., 1780; died, Orleans Co., N. Y., 1863.
JEREMIAH, born, Exeter, R. I., 1782; died, Nassau, N. Y., 1873.
SIMON, born, Exeter, R. I., 1784; died, Nassau, N. Y., 1873.
POLLY, born, Exeter, R. I., 1786; died, Nassau, N. Y., 1835.
DAVID, born, Exeter, R. I., 1788; died, Vetuna, N. Y., 1854.
NANCY, born, Exeter, R. I., 1790; died, Lebanon, N. Y., 1844.
CHARITY, born, Exeter, R. I., 1792; died, Stephentown, N.Y., 1838.
JOHN, born, Nassau, N. Y., 1795; died, Buffalo, N. Y., 1868.
SPRAGUE, born, Nassau, N. Y., 1800; died, April 28, 1896.
JOSEPH, born, Nassau, N. Y., 1802; died, Nassau, N. Y., 1879.
GEORGE W., born, Nassau, N.Y., 1805; died, Buffalo, N. Y., 1882.
CHILDREN OF JOHN AND ANNA TIFFT.

End.

John Tifft removed from Exeter, R. I., to Nassau, N. Y., in Feb. 1793, with his wife and eight children, one span of horses, two yoke of oxen, and farm stock.

End.

JOHN
The son of Robert.
" " " John.
" " " John.
" " " Samuel.
" " " John.
Who was a freeman of Portsmouth, R. I., 1655.

APPENDIX D.

Outline of the ancestors of Marion S. Lamb, wife of Edwin Vallett Tifft, as given by herself.

First Generation.

Isaac Lamb and his father settled first, after coming from England to America, on a large tract of land in Haverhill, New Hampshire, from which they were driven by the Indians, and for safety, they went to Connecticut. In 1696 Isaac Lamb became a freeman and purchased land, in Groton, Conn., 50 acres, of Peter Crary. He lived on this farm 18 years. In 1714 he bought 200 acres in Mystic, Conn. This purchase became the homestead, and has been occupied by his descendants for over 180 years. Isaac Lamb is said to have been a soldier in Cromwell's army. He was one of the founders of the first Baptist Church in Connecticut, and he died in 1723.

Isaac Lamb and Lydia had nine children.

Second Generation.

Isaac Lamb, born in 1705 in Mystic, Conn. It is recorded that his brother Daniel was a teacher. The baptism of two of his sisters is recorded as occurring in 1695 and 1698 in Stonington, Conn. His brother Ezekial had a son who was a Baptist deacon in Holyoke, Mass., and his brother Daniel a son who was a deacon in a Baptist Church. He married Tabitha Wightman, who was the daughter of the Rev. Timothy Wightman. Two of his sons were Baptist clergymen.

Isaac Lamb married Lydia Richards of Preston, Conn., in June, 1733. They had six children. Daniel, their third son, moved to Camillus, N. Y., from Eastern, N. Y.

Third Generation.

Daniel Lamb was a deacon in the Baptist Church of Camillus, N. Y. He had seven children and lived to be 80 years of age—a long life "full of good works."

Fourth Generation.

Isaac Lamb, born in 1778, died in 1843. He married Serena Moore in Stillwater, N. Y. They had two children, Daniel and Henry, their mother dying soon after the birth of Henry.

Fifth Generation.

Daniel Lamb, born June 28, 1809. He married July 7, 1833, in Lebanon, N. Y., to Lydia Groves, who was born Feb. 3, 1814, and who was the daughter of John and Percy Lily Groves, of Lebanon, N. Y.

Lydia Groves Lamb died June 29, 1849, in Lebanon, Madison Co., N. Y. They had five children:

Marion Serena, born Aug. 4, 1835, in Lebanon, N. Y.

Lewis Moore, born Nov. 4, 1837, in Jordon, N. Y.

Marietta Latetia, born Sept. 14, 1843, in Lebanon, N. Y.

DeWitt Groves, born June 16, 1849, in Oneida, N. Y.

Marion Serena Lamb married Edwin V. Tifft.

Daniel Lamb married the second time July 20, 1853, in Hornellsville, N. Y., by Rev. T. S. Sheardown, to Lorinda Dilldine of Hornellsville, N. Y. They had five children.

Daniel Lamb went from Hornellsville, N. Y., to Toledo, Ohio, where he lived 25 years, and from there to Roscommon, Mich., where he died Sept. 30, 1886.

From the Roscommon *News*:—"Mr. Lamb was well known as a temperance worker and was universally esteemed by our citizens."

From the Toledo *Blade*:—"Mr. Lamb was a great worker in the cause of temperance, and his kindly face and winning ways will be sadly missed by his numerous friends."

His oldest child well remembers—when but five years of age—hearing him plead with a man of drinking habits to give them up, while the tears streamed down his face. He became a member of the organization of the Sons of Temperance at their inception and remained in the order till the close of his residence in Toledo, Ohio.

Sixth Generation.

Lewis Moore Lamb, married June 12, 1863, in Friendship, N. Y., to Mary Grace Willard. He enlisted at the beginning of the Civil War, May 16, 1861, in the 23rd Regiment, Col. Hoffman commanding. He was in the battles of Rappahannock Station, Sulphur Springs, Second Bull Run, Chantilly, Antietam, South Mountain and Fredericksburg, and was honorably discharged May 22, 1863, in Elmira, N. Y.

Residence, Friendship, N. Y.

Seventh Generation.

Edwin Willard Lamb, married June 11, 1849, in Wellsville, N. Y., to Harriet Sisson, who was born Jan. 15, 1878, in Wellsville, N. Y.

Residence, Danbury, Conn.

APPENDIX E.

Outline of the Paternal Ancestors of Maria E. (Maxon) Tifft.

First Generation.

Richard Maxson of Boston, Mass., and Portsmouth, R. I., married Goodwife ——. He was a blacksmith. Oct. 1634, he was admitted to the church, being at this time in the employ of James Everill. 1638, Portsmouth. He and others were admitted as inhabitants of the Island of Aquidneck, having submitted themselves to the government that is or shall be established. 1639, Feb. 7. "Richard Maxson, blacksmith, upon complaints made against him, was accordingly detected for his oppression in the way of his trade, who being convinced thereof, promised amendment and satisfaction."

1639, April 30. He and 28 others signed the following compact:

"We whose names are underwritten, do acknowledge ourselves the legal subjects of his majesty King Charles, and in his name do hereby bind ourselves into a civil body politicke, unto his laws according to matters of justice."

1640, March 6. He had 36 acres recorded.

Second Generation.

John Maxson of Newport and Westerly, the first white child born in Rhode Island, near the present site of the city of Newport, in 1639. Died in 1720, Dec. 17. Married Mary Mosher, who was born in 1640, and died Feb. 2, 1718, and the daughter of Hugh Mosher.

On March 22, 1661, he signed certain articles in regard to Misquamicut (Westerly) lands. He became a freeman in 1668, and in 1670-86-90-1705, served as Deputy. October 24, 1677, he was excused from serving on jury because his mother-in-law and wife were both sick. In 1687 he was Overseer of the Poor, and was chosen in this year, with another, to present a petition to Sir Edmund Andros for a town charter. In 1687 and 1688 he served on the Grand Jury. On Sept. 16, 1690, he and two others were appointed by the Assembly to proportion a rate for Westerly. On March 28, 1692, he had a grant of 50 acres near Captain Joseph Davol's, which he sold the next year to Edward Larkin. In March, 1702, he was one of the proprietors in common lands at Newport.

In 1707, June 25, he deeded son Jonathan, for love, etc., 22 acres of land. Sept. 20, 1708 Elder of the Seventh Day Baptist Church.

"Our beloved brother John Maxson, Sr., was ordained to the office of an elder to the congregation in and about Westerly."

Will—proved 1721, Feb. 16. Executors, three sons, John, Joseph and Jonathan. To wife £40, two cows, with keep of same, and the house we now live in to be her abode for life. To son John £5, an iron kettle, and great bible which was my father's. To son Joseph, husbandry tools, riding mare and £5. To son Jonathan, 20s. To daughter Hannah Maxson, a feather bed. To grandsons John, son of John, John, son of Joseph, and John, son of Johnathan, 20s each. To son Joseph's five daughters, viz.: Tacy, Judith, Mary, Ruth and Elizabeth Maxson, each 10s. To daughter Mary Lewis, £12. To children of deceased daughter, Dorothy Clarke, each 40s, viz.: to Freegift, Dorothy, Experience and Joseph.

Inventory: Mare, colt, bonds, wearing apparel, bible, books, including "Doolittle on Sacrament," feather beds, warming pan, pewter, etc.

Third Generation.

John Maxson of Westerly, married Judith Clarke, daughter of Joseph and Bethiah (Mumford) Clarke.

John Maxson, born 1667, died July 1748.

Judith (Clarke) Maxson, born Oct. 12, 1667.

1712, Aug. 21, ordained as Deacon of Seventh Day Baptist Church.

1716, Freeman.

1719, July 5, ordained as Elder.

1748, July 25, inventory. £277, 5s, 4d, viz: pocketbook, money and wearing apparel, £34, 1s., 4d.; books and gloves, £1, 7s., cow-heifer, parts of bible, Josephus' History, part of a warming pan, part of a spinning wheel, 7 sheep, old mare, calf, 2 wether sheep, £20 due next Christmas for sheep, &c. Administration to Captain John Maxson, who took receipts in the next year from his sisters' husbands, and from his nephew Joseph.

Fourth Generation.

John Maxson, born April 21, 1701. Married Thankful Randall.

Fifth Generation.

David Maxson, born July 24, 1729, married Abigail Greeman. He was deputy in General Assembly of Rhode Island. Providence Plantation from Westerly, 1781.

David Maxson was appointed from Westerly to procure and receive the town's proportion of powder, lead and bullets &c.

Sixth Generation.

Asa Maxson, born 1750, March 6, died 1842, Nov. 18. Married Lois Stillman, daughter of Joseph Stillman, born 1756 and died 1820. Buried at Adams Centre, N. Y.

Asa Maxson was Ensign of the 3rd Company of Militia from Westerly, R. I., 1776, 1779, 1780 and 1781. Lieutenant of 3rd Company Militia, Westerly, 1783.

Asa and David Maxson (probably brothers) settled in Petersburg, N. Y., buying 150 acres of land at 5 shillings an acre.

Seventh Generation.

Joseph Stillman Maxon, born Aug. 3, 1797, deacon Seventh Day Baptist Church. He married, Feb. 21, 1822, Elizabeth Vars, who was born Feb. 22, 1802, in Berlin, N. Y. She died in Grand Rapids, Mich., Jan. 31, 1884, and was buried at Adams Centre, N. Y. Joseph Stillman Maxson died Jan. 23, 1836; buried at Adams Centre, N. Y.

Elizabeth Vars descends from John De Vars, whose ancestors can be traced 700 years, back to the nobility of France. John De Vars was born in France about 1650-55; came to America about 1680, and settled at Newport, Rhode Island. He had one child, Isaac De Vars. Isaac had a son, Theodaty. Theodaty had a son, Isaac. Isaac had a son, Thomas, who was the father of Elizabeth (Vars) Maxon.

Eighth Generation.

Thomas Vars Maxon, born March 26, 1823, in Petersburgh, N. Y., married Alma Ann Hull, Oct. 3, 1849, in Berlin, N. Y., by Rev. James Scott, Seventh Day Baptist minister.

Alma Ann (Hull) Maxon died Nov. 3, 1869, in Adams, N. Y.

Thomas Vars Maxon resides in Adams, N. Y.

Ninth Generation.

Maria Elizabeth Maxon, born June 5, 1856, in Adams, N. Y. Married to Wrilson S. Tifft, of Buffalo, N. Y., July 5, 1874, in Adams, N. Y., by Rev. H. W. Bennett.

Tenth Generation.

Maxon Wrilson Tifft, born March 24, 1875, in Buffalo, N.Y.

Lilian Vary Tifft, born June 28, 1877, in Buffalo, N. Y.; died May 16, 1888.

Robert Hull Tifft, born June 23, 1886.

Outline of the Maternal Ancestors of Maria E. (Maxon) Tifft.

First Generation.

George Hull came from Derbyshire, England, in 1633. Was a freeman of Dorchester, Mass., and a representative to the General Assembly. He moved to Windom, Conn., and afterwards to Fairfield. Was Assistant Governor of that state in 1637. George Hull was on committee at the general court, Hartford, Ct., in 1639, when the first constitution in this country was formed.

Second Generation.

Cornelius Hull married Rebecca, daughter of Rev. John Joanes, the first minister of Fairfield, who was of Welch origin.

Third Generation.

Cornelius Hull.

Fourth Generation.

Ebenezer Hull. He must have come to Redding, Conn., prior to 1733, for his name appears in a petition to fix a site for a meeting house in 1725. Ebenezer Hull and wife were among the original church members in 1733.

Fifth Generation.

Daniel Hull, born in Redding, Conn., in the year 1722; died in Berlin, N. Y., Aug. 26, 1811. Mary Betts, his wife, was born in 1728. They removed to Berlin, N. Y., in 1770, and were the first Yankee settlers of that town. They had ten children. Daniel Hull served in the Revolutionary War. The first assembly for religious worship in the town of Berlin was held at Daniel Hull's. In the early history of the town, before it had a code of laws, and being remote from Fort Orange (Albany) the inhabitants chose Daniel Hull and James Denison as a Vigilance Committee, with about the same rights and duties that magistrates now possess. Later, as communication with the outer world was established, he was appointed magistrate with two others, for the entire County of Rensselaer.

When the Declaration of Independence was received the inhabitants through this country assembled at the house of Daniel Hull to hear it read and take counsel for future action. The militia formed in line on the grounds. Here Daniel Hull read that Declaration for the first time, publicly, in the valley of the Hoosick. After the reading he said: "I am one to sustain this Declaration."

Requesting the commanding officer to open ranks he, Daniel Hull, stepping forth between the two lines, requested all who would sustain the Declaration to follow him. Seeing an exciting stir and smile from the soldiers, and looking back he saw his wife, who had joined in the line of march, acknowledging that her services should not be withheld in sustaining that Declaration of Independence.

Sixth Generation.

Daniel Hull, Jr., born in Redding, Conn.; moved with his father to Berlin, N. Y., in 1770; died April 2, 1842. Married Phebe Greene. Held various military offices, to a major's commission, by which title he was generally knowh at the time of

his death. He was a political man of the old school; a Federalist, a frequent member in conventions, representing his people in State and County, and a member of the Legislature. He was a strong advocate of the Freemen's Rights, a promoter of the Arts and Sciences, and a friend of the oppressed.

Seventh Generation.

Benjamin L. Hull, born in Berlin, N. Y., 1796; died in Berlin, Jan. 12, 1869. He married Maria Jones, who was born in 1803. Maria (Jones) Hull was the daughter of James Jones and Waty Jerome. James Jones was the son of James Jones and Catherine Denison. James Jones enlisted from Stephentown, N. Y., in the Revolutionary War. He was on duty a greater portion of the time from the commencement to the close of the war. He was at St. Johns, Ticonderoga, Crown Point, Fort Edward, and other places on Lake George and Lake Champlain as an Orderly Sergeant and also as an Ensign and Lieutenant in Col. Killian Van Rensselaer's regiment of the militia at Albany, Schenectady, Schoharie and other places on the Mohawk River.

Maria Jones Hull died at Newark, N. Y., Jan. 8, 1883, and was buried at Berlin, N. Y.

Eighth Generation.

Alma Ann Hull, born in Berlin, N. Y., March 16, 1829. Married Thomas Vars Maxon, Oct. 3, 1849, in Berlin, N. Y., by Rev. James Scott.

Alma Ann (Hull) Maxon died in Adams, N. Y., Nov. 3, 1869.

Thomas Vars Maxon resides in Adams, N. Y.

Ninth Generation.

Maria Elizabeth Maxon, born June 5, 1856, in Adams, N. Y., and married, July 5, 1874, to Wrilson Simon Tifft, who was born Jan. 10, 1815, in Nassau, N. Y.

Tenth Generation.

Maxon Wrilson Tifft, born March 24, 1875, in Buffalo, N.Y.

Lilian Vary Tifft, born June 28. 1877, in Buffalo, N. Y.; died May 16, 1888.

Robert Hull Tifft, born June 23, 1886.

INDEX.

INDEX.

A

B

ERRATA.

Page 45. 218 should be 213. III Henry R.[9]

Page 75. The generation number should all be one higher commencing with Ann Mary 9.

Page 83. 428 III. should read Priscilla.

Page 115. Joseph is omitted from Nancy and Paul Palmer's family.

Page 121. Should read Rhuel, child of Emma and Mage Milliman.

Page 111. 195 should be 198 VIII Charity.[7]

Page 144, at bottom of. The correct name is George Tift.

Page 105. Charles William and Edwin V. Dufur should be placed with the children of Emily F. and Leonard E. Dufur.

Page 138. Cabel Lewis Teft, should read Cabel Lewis, Left.

www.ingramcontent.com/pod-product-compliance
Lightning Source LLC
Chambersburg PA
CBHW021212270326
41929CB00010B/1093

* 9 7 8 3 7 4 4 7 2 7 0 1 3 *